PRACTICAL SOCIAL WORK

Series Editor: Jo Campling

Editorial Advisory Board:
Robert Adams, Terry Bamford, Charlie Barker, Lena Dominelli, Malcolm Payne, Michael Preston-Shoot, Daphne Statham, and Jane Tunstill

Social work is at an important stage in its development. All professions must be responsive to changing social and economic conditions if they are to meet the needs of those they serve. This series focuses on sound practice and the specific contribution which social workers can make to the well-being of our society in the 1990s.

The British Association of Social Workers has always been conscious of its role in setting guidelines for practice and in seeking to raise professional standards. The conception of the Practical Social Work series arose from a survey of BASW members to discover where they, the practitioners in social work, felt there was the most need for new literature. The response was overwhelming and enthusiastic, and the result is a carefully planned, coherent series of books. The emphasis is firmly on practice, set in a theoretical framework. The books will inform, stimulate and promote discussion, thus adding to the further development of skills and high professional standards. All the authors are practitioners and teachers of social work, representing a wide variety of experience.

JO CAMPLING

Robert Adams
Self-Help, Social Work and Empowerment

David Anderson
Social Work and Mental Handicap

Robert Brown, Stanley Bute and Peter Ford
Social Workers at Risk

Alan Butler and Colin Pritchard
Social Work and Mental Illness

Roger Clough
Residential Work

David M. Cooper and David Ball
Social Work and Child Abuse

Veronica Coulshed
Management in Social Work

Veronica Coulshed
Social Work Practice: An introduction (2nd edn)

Paul Daniel and John Wheeler
Social Work and Local Politics

Peter R. Day
Sociology in Social Work Practice

Lena Dominelli
*Anti-Racist Social Work:
A Challenge for White Practitioners and Educators*

Celia Doyle
Working with Abused Children

Geoff Fimister
Welfare Rights Work in Social Services

Kathy Ford and Alan Jones
Student Supervision

Alison Froggatt
Family Work with Elderly People

Danya Glaser and Stephen Frosh
Child Sexual Abuse

Gill Gorell Barnes
Working with Families

Jalna Hanmer and Daphne Statham
*Women and Social Work:
Towards a Woman-Centred Practice*

Tony Jeffs and Mark Smith
Youth Work

Michael Kerfoot and Alan Butler
Problems of Childhood and Adolescence

Mary Marshall
Social Work with Old People (2nd edn)

Paula Nicolson and Rowan Bayne
Applied Psychology for Social Workers (2nd edn)

Kieran O'Hagan
Crisis Intervention in Social Services

Michael Oliver
Social Work with Disabled People

Lisa Parkinson
Separation, Divorce and Families

Malcolm Payne
Social Care in the Community

Malcolm Payne
Working in Teams

John Pitts
Working with Young Offenders

Michael Preston-Shoot
Effective Groupwork

Carole R. Smith
Adoption and Fostering: Why and How

Carole R. Smith
*Social Work with the Dying
and Bereaved*

Carole R. Smith, Mary T. Lane and
Terry Walshe
Child Care and the Courts

Alan Twelvetrees
Community Work (2nd edn)

Hilary Walker and Bill Beaumont (eds)
Working with Offenders

FORTHCOMING TITLES

Jim Barber
Social Work Practice

Lynne Berry, Crescy Cannan and Karen Lyons
Social Work in Europe

Suzy Braye and Michael Preston-Shoot
Practising Social Work Law

Suzy Croft and Peter Beresford
Involving the Consumer

Angela Everitt et al
Applied Research for Better Practice

Michael Freeman
The Children's Act 1989

David Hebblewhite and Tom Leckie
Social Work with Addictions

Paul Henderson and David Francis
Working with Rural Communities

Rosemary Jefferson and Mike Shooter
Preparing for Practice

Jeremy Kearney and Dave Evans
A Systems Approach to Social Work

Joyce Lishman
Communication and Social Work

Carole Lupton (ed)
Working with Violence

Graham McBeath and Stephen Webb
The Politics of Social Work

Ruth Popplestone and Cordelia Grimwood
Women and Management

Steven Shardlow
Practice: Learning and Teaching

Gill Stewart and John Stewart
Social Work and Housing

Crisis Intervention in Social Services

Kieran O'Hagan

MACMILLAN

First published 1986 by
MACMILLAN EDUCATION LTD
Houndmills, Basingstoke, Hampshire RG21 2XS
and London
Companies and representatives
throughout the world

ISBN 0–333–37668–4 (hardcover)
ISBN 0–333–37669–2 (paperback)

A catologue record for this book is available
from the British Library.

Printed in Hong Kong

Reprinted 1990, 1991

To Maura, Paul, Christine and Brian,
reliable companions in life's crises

Contents

Acknowledgements   ix

1 Crisis Intervention   1

But whose crisis?   1

2 The Crisis Challenge   7

Crisis: a pleasurable, exciting and dramatic
    entertainment   7
Responses to the crisis challenge   9
    Intake teams   9
    Emergency duty teams: a recognised and
        established crisis service   10
    What makes a truly effective crisis service?   11
    Conclusion: a fresh start   12

3 The Crisis Heritage   14

The task of definition   14
America, psychiatry, the sixties   15
    Hope, optimism and confidence   15
The pioneers   17
    Gerald Caplan   17
    The origins of family crisis intervention   20
    The social services crisis context   21
    Conclusion   22

4 Reflections: a Crisis Learning Experience   24

Introductory lessons   24
The agency context: post-Seebohm chaos   25
Divide and conquer   25
'Rescuing' clients from the crisis situation   27

The agency: ally or foe?   29
   The conflictual nature of crisis   29
Crisis referrals   30
   Inaccuracies, misunderstandings and dangers   30
Social services crises   33
Conclusion   34
The impact of different crises upon an
   inexperienced untrained worker (Table 4.1)   35

5 The Plea-for-Removal Crises   40

Definition   40
The characteristics   41
Intervention: making the crisis worse   41
The shaping of perceptions   43
The clamour for removal: the professionals   44
The clamour for removal: the community   45
Plea-for-removal: a 'dumping' crisis?   46
Plea-for-removal: unrecognised suffering and
   care   48
Plea-for-removal: the diminishing options   51
Conclusion   53

6 A New Foundation for Crisis Training   55

Introduction   55
Family therapy   55
Common goals in family therapy and crisis intervention   56
Towards a new theory of crisis for social workers   58
   Family therapy theories   58
Deriving a theory of crisis from systems theory   61
   The crisis system   61
   Closed and unhealthy 'open' systems   62
Struggle and conflict in crisis   63
   Morphostasis and morphogenesis   63
   The application of the theory   66
Clients' perceptions in crisis situations   69
Perceptual intervention   69
Self-knowledge in crisis situations   71
   Social work principles and crisis realities   71
   An unexpected development   71

The unpleasantness of crisis situations 73
Professional and moral vulnerability in crisis
    intervention 74
A conceptual framework for exploration 74
Conclusion 81

7 **'I Don't Want to Lose My Baby'** **82**

Introduction 82
The crisis referral 83
Initial reaction and first contact 84
    Analysis and comment (1) 86
    Systems perspective (1) 86
    Moral and professional vulnerability (1) 88
Replacing the crisis system: space, balance and
    order 89
    Analysis and comment (2) 92
    Systems perspective (2) 93
    Moral and professional vulnerability (2) 94
Strengthening the new system: a shift in focus 97
    Analysis and comment (3) 97
The 'heart' of the matter 98
    Analysis and comment (4) 99
    The therapeutic potential in crisis 101
Crisis resolution 101

8 **Ethical Considerations for Crisis Intervention** **105**

Introduction 105
Powerful social worker powerless client! 105
The ugly face of crisis 107
    The inalienable rights of whom? 107
    Violence in crisis situations 109
Power, authority and control in crisis situations 110
    Source and use 110
    Manipulation 112
    Statutory removal 113
Impediments in training for crisis intervention 114
    The 'oppressed', 'innocent' client! 114
    Implications for clients in crisis 117

Conclusion 119

9 Social Services: the Organisational Context **121**

Introduction: model enterprises and all that 121
Crisis intervention: the challenge for
management 122
A wealth of experience 122
Establishing the facts 122
Social worker's limitations for crisis work 124
Respecting and responding to the worker's
limitations 124
Crisis intervention and staff supervision 125
Knowledge: the crisis context 125
Recording: a crucial learning tool 127
Supervision: ethical considerations 127
Senior management and crisis intervention 128
Accepting the realities 128
Supervision: the task for senior management 129
Crisis policies compatible with crisis principles 130
Other agencies' perceptions of crisis intervention
in social services 132
Conclusion 133

10 Crisis Intervention **136**

But whose crisis? 136
Self-exploration : the unending search 138
Crisis intervention : the real meaning 140

Bibliography 143

Index 150

Acknowledgements

I am indebted to friends and colleagues throughout North Yorkshire; in particular, to the Selby team, past and present members. The conceptual frameworks in Chapters 4 and 6 presented special typing difficulties in the original manuscripts, but, as always, Silvia Mileham's kindness and resourcefulness came to the rescue.

The knowledge and experience upon which the book is based has been gained principally through the crisis experiences of my clients in Selby. Though all of them may not be aware of it, their contribution to this book is immeasurable.

In this book, there are many descriptions of varying length and detail, about actual crisis cases. Great care has been taken in the attempt to conceal the identities of the clients in question. Names, places, and time, have been significantly altered, and certain material facts have been omitted. The experiences of the social worker in dealing with these crises, however, are exactly as described.

KIERAN O'HAGAN

1

Crisis Intervention

But whose crisis?

1974. There really was not any need for a doctor's opinion, according to the referrer; this was quite clearly a non-accidental injury. But the doctor would be called anyhow. Procedure demanded it, and more importantly, the child, David, might need treatment. I left the office to see this injury for myself, and to investigate the circumstances. I was feeling both determined and confident, yet the journey of ten miles to the village primary school which David attended, became increasingly a lonely and apprehensive one. I was relieved to arrive at the school, to be greeted warmly and briefed by David's teacher and the headmistress. David was a beautiful blond-haired child with sad blue eyes, and a finger locked in his mouth. He was utterly confused by all this attention, but was able to say once again that his dad had punched him.

The child returned to his classroom. Discussion resumed between myself and the headmistress. She knew the family well; the whole village knew the family well; constant bickerings, complaints, drunkenness, police involvement... 'there was no need for it...they had a lovely home...and four lovely children...this was a very peaceful village...'.

The doctor arrived. She diagnosed non-accidental injury saying it had been caused by a hefty punch, but treatment was unnecessary. As I drove to the home, I thought how convenient it would be if this matter could have been investigated entirely at the school, how warm and friendly everyone was. There was nobody at David's home. I sat in the car for a while, pondering, and again feeling lonely and apprehensive. The headmistress had suggested father might be in the village pub. I went there, hoping I would not find him. I returned to the home and waited, certain that either of the parents would turn up within the next thirty minutes. It was now 3.30. Sure enough, about twenty minutes later, a car drew up alongside, its driver and passengers staring at me as they went past. My heart began to beat faster, and when I saw a stocky 6ft 3in. figure accompanied by his wife and children -including David-glancing at me suspiciously as they walked up the garden path, I had the strongest possible urge to run. Then my act began: the confident strident movements getting out of the car, walking upright towards them, hoping to give the appearance of at least an inch more than my modest 5ft 8in. 'Why hadn't I given them time to get in?' I suddenly asked myself, feeling like a gazelle charging in on a pride of lions.

'Are you Mr Walker? I'm from Social Services...can I have a word with you?'

There were two very different reactions: Mrs Walker immediately turned away from me and her hand visibly shook as she tried to get the key into the lock. But Mr Walker stood deadly still, looking down on me with ice-cold eyes full of aggression. I too now wanted to be inside, I wanted to be seated, preferably in an armchair for maximum support, and my trembling knees steadied by my legs crossed. But Mr Walker would not oblige; although he beckoned me in, he then quickly turned on me with a silent demand that I identify myself and my purpose.

Good God...what do I say to him? 'Mr Walker, I want to talk to you about your son...Mr and Mrs Walker, I/we/Social Services have been informed...I wonder have either of you any idea why I'm here... Mr Walker, it's my duty to...This is a lovely home you have...Can I speak to you alone Mr Walker...Can I speak to both of you alone... Would you mind asking the children to go into another room....'

But I said none of these things. 'I'm from Social Services Mr Walker', was as much as I could manage.

The two older children Deborah (13) and Mark (12) remained close to their mother; I could see they resented me and that mother was frightened of me. Strangely enough, David virtually ignored me, choosing instead to get down to some telly and Lego simultaneously. He was joined by his younger sister Carol.

These were cruel distractions, I thought, to be ignored, resented and feared in this way. The television made matters worse. I had come to confront Mr Walker, but now a multitude of sounds, movements, looks, thoughts and feelings were bearing down upon me.

'Oh yea, an' what's that about?' Mr Walker said quite sharply.

'Your son, David. He had a large bruise on the side of his head. He's been seen by a doctor. It was done by...!'

Mrs Walker yelled out. I did not hear what she said, but it was obvious that every word I had spoken had increased her agitation. She charged in and out of the room repeatedly, yelling abuse at me, yet with a terrified look in her eyes. She had a powerful pair of lungs and the loudest piercing voice that quickly rendered 'Playtime' inaudible, and had the two younger children scrambling to their feet and rushing to her side in utter panic. 'Mammy mammy! What's wrong... What's that man doing mammy?' they screamed, as they clutched her waist and stared petrified at me. 'It's all right, loves' she said, making an attempt to embrace both of them, with clenched fists, and then continuing her tirade against me, which only made them clutch her more tightly. Only Mr Walker could effectively interrupt this pandemonium.

'I did it,' he said.

'I made him do it,' cried his wife. Just when I thought that I was going to be engulfed in a sea of passion and hysteria, I now found myself equally impotent before these entirely unexpected utterances of confession and loyalty. The most conflicting and confusing impressions came to mind: the child had been injured and should be removed; but perhaps it was highly exceptional in this lovely home and loyal family, and the child should not be removed; maybe it had only the appearance of a lovely home and loyal family, and this hysteria and passion was a manifestation of something more sinister, as was that ugly bruise on David's head. Our office had been showered with memos and circulars during the last few months, and there was our green booklet on non-accidental injury stating unequivocally that David should be removed; but how in the name of God was David going to be removed?

'Can you tell me what happened?' I asked, biding time in the hope of some deliverance from the utter chaos and uncertainty of my mind.

Mr Walker had hit David because he was driving mother demented last night and she had begged her husband to do something before she 'cracked up'. Mr Walker had been papering in one of the bedrooms and the increasingly noisy but hollow threats by his wife were getting on his nerves too. When she actually came up to seek his help that was the last straw.

I believed every word of this. I looked at the tense taut face of Mrs Walker and recalled her loud piercing voice, and I sympathised with Mr Walker. My attention drifted back to David, with the simultaneous thoughts that he was perhaps in some danger, but that it would be one helluva job to remove him from that danger. Then I was told something else that gave rise to a modicum of resolve: 'Mr Walker' and 'Mrs Walker' were not married. Mr Walker was not the father of David. The couple had been co-habiting for many years, each having two children by their former partners. David most certainly was in danger, I then thought, and should be removed. But how to regain authority when they'd already sensed my feebleness?

'Mr Walker, I have to tell you you've committed a serious offence.

'What offence?'

'You've caused an injury to a child.'

'One smack?' he said with forced contempt, suddenly provoking in my mind the possibly ugly spectacle of a sustained attack leading up to that injury. I wanted to reply to his contempt by saying he could kill a child with one smack, but I was scared.

'Quite a heavy smack, Mr Walker. It left a large bruise which you can still see.'

As I spoke and stared straight at him, I was forever conscious of the impact upon his wife. She was tensing again, fidgeting, tightening her grip around the two younger children.

'What do you want to do about it?' he asked.

The crunch question. The one I dreaded, to be avoided by the typically semantic 'professional' escape, unburdening me of all responsibility: 'It's not a question of me wanting anything, Mr Walker; it's what the law says.'

'What does the law say?'

I knew I dared not hesitate. I replied immediately. 'There's a Place of Safety Order being prepared for a Magistrate to sign right now. David will be taken to a place of safety for a short while, until this matter is investigated.'

The result was predictable, but more hysterical and frightening than before. Mrs Walker seemed to lose all control, exposing her two youngest children by removing her arms from around them, and biting deep into the knuckles of one hand at the same time as she tried to force out a panic-ridden cry. Then she stormed out of the room and back again, hurling abuse and invoking the heavens to rescue her. The children sought refuge around Mr Walker. Even the older two held onto him, and their resentment of me turned into hatred and fear. For the first time I could hear the nervous tremors in Mr Walker's voice when he said: 'Over my dead body.'

It was at this point that a rapidly growing suspicion in my mind turned into a harsh fact: I had made matters worse and was quite capable of precipitating some catastrophe that would render the cause of my enquiry, David's bruise, an irrelevancy. Yet I had to do something. I would have to be firm, gain a grip on the situation, perhaps talk about child abuse procedures which would have to be adhered to whether they liked it or not; or say to him that he had the opportunity of co-operating with me, or running the risk of committing more serious offences. Firmness, without further provocation, that was what was needed. But how? I could maybe pacify and reassure them that I was not removing David for ever; that I wanted to help them by exploring the relationship tensions which had led up to this incident; that I could recognise that despite that incident they had achieved a great deal, as was demonstrated this very moment in their beautiful home, by their love and loyalty to each other, and by their reactions to me.

But as such thoughts ran through my mind, there was also the nagging doubt about their sincerity. Did I really mean all that? Did I believe it? I imagined myself saying such things and they sounded insincere and daft; I realised they were symptomatic of my own crisis, and no part of a strategy for dealing with theirs. So I said nothing, compelled instead to listen to Mr Walker's protestations about the triviality of the bruising and the extremity of my intentions. And he punctuated whatever he was saying with the same threat: 'Over my dead body.'

Suddenly, Mrs Walker intervened in a way that I could never have anticipated. She rushed towards David. She got down on her knees and clutched his little shoulders. She looked into his frightened eyes and said: 'This man's come to take you away darling, do you want to go?' David flung his arms around her and screamed 'No!' She held him back off her and said: 'He's taking you away because Daddy beat you last night... What did he beat you for, darling?' David could not reply. He tried to fling his arms around her again but she still held him off. 'You love daddy, don't you darling?' she asked. 'Yes, yes...' the child screamed. 'You don't want to be taken away from him by this man, do you?' He yelled the reply she needed, and then she relented and allowed him to bury his head over her neck, his tear-laden face out of my sight. His mother did not hide her face. She looked up at me and stared at me, patting her child on the back at the same time. The whole family stared at me, each of them now in close physical contact. 'Just leave us alone,' said Mrs Walker. 'We don't need you!'

2
The Crisis Challenge

Crisis: a pleasurable, exciting and dramatic entertainment

The principal recurring theme in all forms of literature, music and art is the struggle between good and evil, between the vulnerability and the potential of the human condition. That struggle is manifest in crisis; crises within the individual; or between the individual and his family, community, nation and God. It is a stirring theme, based not upon mere imaginative fancy, but on actual life experiences. Our lives are surrounded by crises, local, national, international, which are equally thought-provoking, even entertaining; always characterised by the drama of the action, the passionate involvement of the protagonists, and the unpredictability of the outcome. Such fact and fiction combined determine both perception and response to crisis, and herein lies the first of many paradoxes: that crisis learning is immensely popular amongst social workers and students, yet social workers are extremely reluctant to become involved in crisis situations, particularly crises of the mentally ill (Clark, 1971). Social work educators seem unaware of this paradox and the reasons for it. They devise and prepare papers on crisis intervention which are avidly read, and crisis courses which are always heavily over-subscribed. But they are unaware of, or indifferent, or helpless, in the face of their student's deeply embedded fears of many of the characteristics of crisis (Jordan and Packman, 1978). This paradox may have something to do with a credibility gap, the fact that very few educators have any more enthusiasm for crisis work than their students, and no more experience. If social work students are, generally speaking, middle class, and have little experience of the crisis situations of clients, then their tutors, closeted for many years in university lecture theatres and offices, are not the ideal personnel for grappling with the fears generated by crisis situations which they themselves could not face, let alone solve. But this raises the question: why are students still eager to learn about crises from educators who have little or no training, competence or experience in crisis intervention? The regrettable fact is that the popularity of crisis learning is rooted more in the universal perception of crisis as a pleasurable, exciting and dramatic entertainment, than in a desire to embroil oneself in real-life crisis situations with the express intention of solving them. Even the words themselves, 'crisis' and 'crisis intervention' sparkle midst the doldrums of 'IT', 'welfare rights', the '1983 Mental Health Act', and so on; they evoke thought and feeling more akin to the pleasures derived from literary creation than to the fears and apprehensions provoked by certain crisis responsibilities. All the conditions of entertainment are fully satisfied in the crisis learning component of social work training; aimiable company, pleasant surroundings, a fascinating topic, stimulating discussion and humour, and above all, the conspicuous absence of the kind of challenges which arise in crisis work. In this priviliged setting, the world of crisis is dissected with a confidence and enthusiasm which will dissipate rapidly the nearer one gets to a real-life crisis situation. The crisis under discussion will always be someone else's crisis in some far distant location, a fantasy world in comparison with the frightening reality of a statutory obligation which declares that this crisis is in your own backyard and you had better do something about it quickly. Role play and video recording are the order of the day, enhancing the entertainment value and certain to provoke the occasional rapturous fits of giggling, but few social workers laugh in the midst of a crisis. The consequence of all this is plain to see: instead of an awareness and preparation for the cruelty, suffering and danger which are at the heart of many crisis situations and which can be as damaging to the worker as to the client, students emerge from the college with the conviction that crisis learning has been a most interesting and rewarding part of the course (Gorrell Barnes, 1980). Many pay dearly for their awakening out of that woeful inadequacy of training.

Responses to the crisis challenge

Intake teams

How have social services departments responded to the fact that newly qualified social workers are totally ill prepared for crisis intervention work? The development of 'Intake' teams would appear to be a major positive response. These teams are fundamentally a 'front line' unit, in which the worker is expected to encounter far more crisis situations, and to be more effective in solving them. As Loewenstein (1974) so vividly describes, social services were in general chaos in the immediate post-Seebohm years. This was most obvious in the initial contacts between client and department; anxious angry clients, harassed receptionists, inexperienced workers. The unprincipled results were predictable: workers disliked the duty rota system, regarding it as a nuisance getting in the way of their own cases, and so they arranged for their own clients to 'call in' during their duty rota; they used 'delaying tactics' before seeing other clients; and expected receptionists to ask clients 'intimate details of their problems in public, so that they could arm themselves with some information before actually seeing them' (Loewenstein, p.118).

The establishment of intake teams eradicated many of these problems, but fell far short of creating an effective and professional crisis intervention service. Buckle's (1981) comprehensive study of intakes reveals that such a service was never really the objective: 'the prime motivation was to protect the quality of long-term social work' (p.42). More specifically, the intention was to allow long-term workers to 'undertake planned and preventative work and to do intensive and experimental work without the demands of shot term and crisis work' (p.42). It is not surprising then to learn from Buckle and Loewenstein that despite being in the 'front line' of crisis work, intake workers have no crisis training either, nor that very few have any theoretical or conceptual underpinning of their responses to crisis.

Emergency duty teams: a recognised and established crisis service

Emergency duty teams, small teams of very experienced and skilled practitioners ready to intervene in any crisis situation referred to them, and genuinely interested in and highly competent in crisis work, are certainly regarded as an effective crisis service. But, just like intake teams, the origin of EDTs lies more in the inadequacy and rigidity of the immediate post-Seebohm departmental structures, rather than any universal desire on the part of social workers and managers to create an effective crisis service. In the early seventies, the increasingly influential union representatives amongst social workers were acutely aware of the impact of out-of-hours emergency work upon members, in terms of disruption to their personal and family life, and the inadequate amount they were paid for the job. Management was made aware of a growing discontent, which was actually manifested in industrial action in some inner city departments. They were then compelled to question the quality of emergency service being provided by a reluctant, dissatisfied staff. The two largest categories of out-of-hours emergency work are child care and mental health (BASW, 1984) and, regarding the former, management was hypersensitive to criticisms of entirely inadequate social work responses to significant occurrences out-of-hours in numerous child abuse scandals, the most notorious of which was Maria Colwell (DHSS, 1974).

There are two major characteristics in EDTs which should caution anyone who believes they are some kind of high-powered, effective crisis service: 'training' and 'motivation'. Crisis training is virtually non-existent for EDT members. This fact is made repeatedly in BASW's latest report on EDTs (1984); made by the authors, but more importantly, by the workers themselves. Here is an anonymous EDT *leader* on the topic of training:

> The training is really abysmal on lots of points...there seems to be a lack of people who can train night duty workers....The

training officers have no real conception of what its like to do night duty...the training has always been bad. (p.35)

There have been attempts to pretend otherwise. The grandiloquently entitled 'First National Training Conference on Crisis and Emergency Social Work', for example, took place in London in 1982. About 75 per cent of those who attended were EDT workers. If they expected any form of training, or any indication that effective training was going to be made available at some time in the future, they must have been disappointed: the conference consisted of nothing more than twelve formal lectures over a three-day period, delivered in the main by psychiatrists and others having little or no experience of the harsh realities of crisis intervention in social services departments. Thankfully there has not been a second such 'training' conference.

'Motivation' is an entirely different matter. Social workers join EDTs for a variety of reasons. Some may join to acquire or to exercise their experience and competence in crisis work, or to specialise in child care or mental health crisis. But there are sufficient grounds for suggesting a rather more powerful motivating factor: family and domestic commitments, more money, freedom and autonomy; generally, a good deal more convenient for the worker and his immediate family. There is nothing dubious about such motivation, nor should it be a point of criticism. It emerges time and again from the BASW report, reminding us of former colleagues who have joined EDTs and who have told us honestly of the same motivation. But it has to be stressed that crisis intervention often necessitates a selfless and sustained commitment to clients, wholly incompatible with self-interest and convenience.

What makes a truly effective crisis service?

Generic social workers, intake and EDT members have all been subjected to the same inadequacy of crisis training and supervision in crisis work. A truly effective, tested, and reputable crisis training programme does not exist anywhere in this country. The lack of knowledge and experience of crisis intervention in social services on the part of those principally responsible for training, is indicated by the fact that not a single text on the subject has been written in the last twenty years, which have seen a deluge of social work publications. As for the efforts of social services departments, it is quite clear that Intake and EDTs are purely pragmatic responses to various aspects of post-Seebohm chaos, union pressure, and public opinion.

Social workers, social services management, and social work trainers do not have to be reminded that the crisis task in social services constitutes the most formidable and expensive challenge. This text emerges from a conviction strengthened over a decade of social work in one typical social services office: that the potential for surmounting that challenge lies more within the individual worker than in any crisis component of social work training, or type of work and team context in which they will later operate. The vast majority of social workers encounter various forms of crisis each working week and face them alone, irrespective of whether they work in Intake, EDTs, after-hours standby, or in ordinary generic teams. It is the social worker, him or herself, their personal qualities, their self-training, experience, knowledge, skill, integrity, motivation, and, above all else, their level of self-awareness as to their impact on the crisis and vice versa-these are the crucial determinants in the provision of an effective crisis intervention service.

Conclusion: a fresh start

During and after my experience in the previous chapter, I felt I had nothing to offer such a service. I had just completed a two year postgraduate social work course which I had enjoyed immensely, particularly the 'crisis training' component. That was dominated by a highly regarded and established literature produced in the main by American psychiatrists in the sixties. There is a need to start afresh. The following chapter will look at the origins and context of that literature, beginning with the unfinished task of definition of crisis. Chapter 4 will briefly describe crisis experiences in a social services office, and will demonstrate that the British social services crisis context in which social workers may face an infinite variety of crisis situations alone at any time of day or night, is entirely different from that of classical crisis literature. In Chapter 5 the focus will be on a particular category of crisis, those in which a request or demand is made to remove a client. Chapter 6 attempts to lay the foundation for a more relevant and effective crisis training that can meet this challenge. Underpinning the discipline and theory it provides, is a conceptual framework that will enable social workers to explore their own vulnerablities in crisis situations. In Chapter 7, the discipline theory and self-knowledge will be applied in response to a plea-for-removal crisis, typical of many arising in dismembered families, living in multi-deprived communities in those sprawling run-down council estates, in which social workers spend most of their time. Chapter 8 looks at the ethical implications of the family crisis intervention theory and strategy which is being advocated, and argues that the moral and philosophical base constructed for social workers in the late sixties is naïve and inadequate for crisis intervention in social services today. Chapter 9 explores the numerous ways in which social services management can enhance the quality of crisis services provided by individual social workers. Finally, Chapter 10 very briefly describes a recent social work response to a crisis. It is some ten years after the experience recorded in the first chapter. I am confident that this book will enable social workers to intervene in crisis situations far more effectively.

3
The Crisis Heritage

The task of definition

The word 'crisis' has a universal appeal that curiously excludes any enthusiasm for the task of defining it. Classical crisis literature made little progress in this matter, as indicated by its retreat from an earlier unequivocal stance: 'crisis is...',to the safer but more vague: 'a crisis refers to... a crisis occurs when... a crisis effects...crisis has been viewed as... a crisis is provoked by...' (Umana *et al.*, 1980). This led Schulberg and Sheldon (1968) to remark: 'one cannot help but be struck by the arbitrary varying and even elusive qualities currently associated with the term... it remains for the most part diffident in definition, popular in usage, and ambigious in value'(p.554).

The difficulty in defining crisis is obvious. A set of circumstances or conditions which constitute a crisis for one individual, may not do so for another. An unmanageable problem may render Mr Smith in a state of panic, and may be a matter of indifference to Mrs Brown. The sight of a spider could provoke a massive phobic reaction which we may justifiably call a crisis for the person concerned, whilst the birth of a mentally handicapped child may be perfectly manageable to those with strengths we admire and cannot comprehend. Given such inconsistencies and indefinable determinants it is easy to understand why many of the pioneers gave up the task of definition. In research into family crises, Langsley *et al.* (1968a) admitted his frustration and concluded: 'crisis theory has defined the crisis as the hazardous event (stress) and the subsequent reaction to that event' (p.156).

So it is impact which constitutes a crisis, the perceptions and feelings of the individual at the centre of it, and the degree of risk they sense in trying to cope with it. But does not this make crisis experience virtually limitless? It would appear so, and social workers who were students in the sixties and seventies may now cast a critical eye over much of the crisis literature then available. Working in Brixton, for example, a social worker is not likely to benefit from Klein and Ross's (1958) study of American middle-class families facing the 'crisis' of their children entering kindergarten; nor from Le Master's (1957) study of 49 healthy, stable, middle-class, white, graduate couples experiencing the 'crisis' of the birth of their first child. Yet such studies are well established in the annals of crisis literature and research, of little value to social workers in social services departments for obvious reasons, and yet social workers in the sixties and seventies, much to the delight of publishers and authors alike, had to spend much valuable time studying them.

America, psychiatry, the sixties

Hope, optimism and confidence

American psychiatry is the principal source of classical crisis literature. The conceptualisation of 'crisis' and the emergence of crisis intervention as a discipline in its right were the inevitable consequences of increasing doubt about the efficacy of the classical model of long-term psychoanalytic and psychotherapeutic treatment, and of an increasing confidence in the use of brief, action-orientated therapy. The crisis of hospitalisation was a prime target for what became known as preventative community psychiatry. In an era of boundless optimism and novelty, and in a profession rapidly emerging as the most prestigious within medicine, Caplan (1964) had few reservations about psychiatry's ability to immerse itself in the communities it served, to improve the mental health of the masses, and to develop crisis intervention services which would drastically reduce the number of emergency psychiatric admissions. Psychiatrists were henceforth to influence the political, educational, economic and social life of the community. They were in effect to become community politicians, educators and mass communicators, who would be able to influence legislators and administrators for the general good. In the specific area of crisis, it was just not good enough to provide quality crisis intervention services; psychiatrists should be willing to seek out those focal points in a community where crises are likely to arise, such as: 'pre-natal clinics, surgical wards, accident wards, divorce courts, kindergartens, and the first grade of schools, college dormitories at the start of the school year, funeral parlours, and the offices of clergymen. . .' (Caplan, 1964, p.69).

It is important for British social workers to flavour this mood of confidence and optimism in the America of the sixties. British social work never was a profession characterised by dynamic leadership or self-confidence, and the traumas of reorganisation made its educators and management particularly vulnerable to all the prevailing intellectual winds of the day. American psychiatry's feverish activity and output was eagerly seized on this side of the Atlantic by an undiscerning chaotic profession whose own output in the field of crisis intervention in particular, amounted to nothing at all. The post-Seebohm social work educators were 'indebted' to such prominent figures as Lindermann, Caplan, Langsley, and Aguilera *et al.*, American psychiatrists knowing as much about the crisis responsibilities of generic social workers in the emerging British social services departments, as they did about community politics in outer Mongolia. The irony is further heightened by the psychiatric perception of social work. As far back as 1944, Lindermann concluded his classic study of grief reactions, by admitting that not all bereaved persons would be in a position to receive expert psychiatric help, so: 'much of this knowledge will have to be passed on to auxiliary workers. Social workers and ministers will have to be on the lookout for the ominous signs, referring the more disturbed persons to the psychiatrist while assisting those with more normal reactions' (p.19). Aguilera and Messick (1974) spoke of the danger of the 'de-professionalisation of major mental health functions', but recognised that there could be some merit in recruiting other medical professionals along with 'teachers, lawyers, clergy, policemen, firemen, social and welfare workers, and so on' (p.10). Langsley *et al.* (1968a) included a social worker in their famous multidisciplinary crisis team; but whilst Langsley and his medical colleagues embroiled themselves in the drama of mental health crisis, trying to prevent damaging hospitalisation for many, the social worker merely stood on the periphery, ready to step into a role clearly defined by Langsley himself: 'Generally, he is the most knowledgeable member of the team about other social agencies...involved in getting information from these agencies, arranging for inter-agency contact...participating in discharge planning...' (p.40).

This ancillary function of social workers is deeply embedded in the psychiatric unconscious. A few social work writers, notably Rapoport (1962) and Parad (1965) have made an impact in crisis literature, but their contribution has been largely influenced by the psychiatrist crisis pioneer, Caplan (1961, 1964). They make frequent references to him and other crisis pioneering psychiatrists as the principal sources of knowledge and inspiration for their own work.

The pioneers

Gerald Caplan

Caplan is without question the most famous of the pioneers. He produced a unified theory of crisis upon which virtually all models of crisis intervention have relied (1961, 1964). Caplan states that the origin of all crises must be a problem, and 'problem' should therefore be adequately defined.

> The normal consistancy of pattern, or equilibrium, is maintained by homeostatic re-equilibrating mechanisms, so that temporary deviations from the pattern call into operation opposing forces which automatically bring the pattern back to its previous state. In other words, the equilibrium may be said to be upset by the individual or the system being faced by a force or situation which alters its previous function: we call this a 'problem'. (Caplan,1964, p.38)

Normally, there are ways and means of solving a problem, particularly if it has been solved before. One expects then to be able to solve it again, by the same method, in about the same time. The degree of tension and effort involved is quite tolerable. But in a 'crisis' the problem is such that it poses a threat 'to a fundamental need satisfaction ... and the circumstances are such that habitual problem solving methods are unsuccessful within the time span of past expectations of success' (1964, p.44). Tension rises therefore to an extent which causes anxiety, fear, guilt or shame and a feeling of helplessness in the face of the insoluble problem develops, leading to some 'disorganisation of functioning'.

Caplan conceptualises the tension aspects of crisis by outlining four specific phases:

1. The initial rise in tension caused by the problem stimulus.
2. An increase in tension because the problem has not been solved.
3. A further increase compelling the individual to do everything in their power to solve the problem: novel methods of attack; redefining; perceiving hitherto neglected aspects of the problem; giving up trying to solve the whole problem.
4. If the problem continues and can neither be solved with need satisfaction or perceptual distortion, the tension mounts beyond a further threshold or its burden increases over time, to a breaking point; major disorganisation of the individual with drastic results then occurs.

Caplan believed that 'every crisis represents a novel situation, in which novel forces, both internal and external are involved' (1964, p.41). Historical, sociocultural and family context could have a bearing on the outcome of the crisis, and psychiatrists should examine these contexts. Caplan stated that crisis is characteristically self-limiting and that the crisis resolution (equilibrium) for better or worse, occurs within four to six weeks from the onset. He emphasised that the crisis period, despite or because of the pain it caused the individual, was nevertheless a time of opportunity, a situation of therapeutic potential, because as his experiences and researches had demonstrated, persons in crisis are receptive to efforts to help:

> During the disequilibrium of the crisis, a person is more susceptible to influence by others than during periods of stable functioning. When the forces are, as it were teetering in the balance, a relatively minor intervention may weigh them down to one side or the other... Crisis therefore presents care-giving persons with a remarkable opportunity to deploy their efforts to maximum advantage in influencing the mental health of others. (1964, p.48)

This theory of Caplan's had a profound influence on the amount and context of crisis literature and research which followed. Caplan had set a precedent by deducing a theory from his and others' experiences of the impact of situational, maturational and natural disaster crises upon the mental health of the individual. Soon after, there was a deluge of crisis research on every conceivable crisis situation: the crisis of rape, attempted suicide, premature birth, stillborn birth, birth of a handicapped child, national disasters, local disasters, war wounded, war widowed, drug addiction, marriage, divorce, remarriage, reconstituted family, middle age, old age, death in the family, anniversaries of death in the family, etc. Of fundamental importance, of course, from a publishing and eye-catching point of view, was that the titles always contained the word 'crisis'. Within this research and the avalanche of publications which followed, Caplan's theory was always acknowledged and never critically examined, least of all in its application to social work practice. Even twenty years on, significant social work opinion in Britain can still regard Caplan as quite simply 'the best' (Butler and Pritchard, 1983, p.155). But such an opinion refers only to the relevance of Caplan's theory to mental illness and psychiatric emergencies. It should be remembered that Caplan's theory evolved from his conceptual model of preventative community psychiatry. Caplan's use of the term 'crisis' pertains strictly to the mental health or ill health of the client in question: 'In analysing the effect of a crisis in relation to mental disorder....' is a recurring statement in Caplan's exposition of a theory. Social workers are not likely to miss the point. They deal with numerous kinds of crises in which no questions need arise about the mental health or ill health of the individual concerned. Even less may there be a need for a psychiatrist to help solve such crises.

The origins of family crisis intervention

Rapaport (1971) was one of the few early pioneers to admit that the emerging discipline of crisis intervention was lacking in any understanding of the nature of crisis 'as it manifests itself in a family system' and which would have encouraged the development of relevant 'methods and techniques for treatment of the family as a whole' (p.118). This particular challenge was however, being tackled with much publicity in crises associated with emergency psychiatric admissions. The best known and the most widely read of these new family crisis interventionists was the psychiatrist, Donald Langsley. The work of Langsley and his associates at Colorado Psychiatric Hospital provided the family conceptualisations and frameworks for a more credible diagnosis and treatment in mental illness crises. He produced a series of articles based primarily on their highly acclaimed text *The Treatment of Families in Crisis* (1968b) Langsley traced the development of various models of treatment of the mentally ill; from 'patient orientated model' through 'stress orientated model', and finally favouring the 'system (family) orientated model'. Langsley formulated a crisis intervention strategy which is generally held as a model in the field of psychiatric admissions, and which is referred to in virtually every crisis text which followed. Its famous seven steps are fairly concentrated upon the family: immediate aid to all family members caught up in the crisis including medication to calm those most upset; the problem to be defined as a family one; making family members aware of aspects of their family life which have a direct bearing upon the crisis but for which hospitalisation is not necessary; general prescription and blocking of any regressive tactic or trends—this may necessitate continuing and demonstrable reassurance and support; specific prescription in which tasks are assigned for the 'resumption of functioning' and for resolution of the crisis state; negotiation of role conflict; and finally, the management of future crises, in which the family is again assured of the availability of the treatment team (Langsley *et al.*, 1968 b,c; Langsley *et al*, 1971)

Just as Caplan's theory of crisis was followed by a deluge of research and practice publications chiefly by mental health practictioners, Langsley's much broader focus on the family of the client in crisis had a similar effect. The foundations of family crisis intervention were being laid out from a synthesis of strategies developed in crisis intervention and in family therapy. The latter was soon to emerge as the dominant influence in family crisis intervention. In Britain particularly, the focus in crisis intervention was to widen much further still. Bott (1976) and Scott (1974; Scott and Starr, 1981) defined mental health crises not just within the context of the patient and his family, but within the macro view of the hospital itself, the community it serves, and the historical social and political processes and pressures which shape and dictate the nature of psychiatric provision in general , and the responses to the crisis of hospitalisation in particular. Langsley in America, and Scott in England (Barnet) were also pioneers in the creation of highly mobile multidisciplinary crisis teams, the principal aims of which were to enable clients to avoid psychiatric hospitalisation, and to provide the necessary support to the families having to accommodate their mentally ill member.

The social services crisis context

Having looked at this historical and evolutionary context of crisis literature, the question now arises: how useful is it as a principal component part of crisis training in social work courses? There are numerous ways of approaching this query, and a useful starting point may be to offer typical crisis problems which arise today in any social services office.

Teresa is fifteen. She is in a residential home after persistent absconding, glue sniffing, and estrangement from her distinctly middle-class parents and private school. During the last few days relationships between her and the residential staff have deteriorated. The duty officer in charge has phoned the standby duty officer to say that there has been a violent row and that Teresa has locked herself in her room threatening to commit suicide.

Mrs Brown came to the office bruised and distressed. Her cohabitee has beaten her for the umpteenth time. But today he has also beaten the oldest of Mrs Brown's three children. Mrs Brown wants something done immediately. Yet she demands that no one speaks to her cohabitee. She asks the social worker to swear that no one will. When it is pointed out to her that her cohabitee should be interviewed, Mrs Brown become hysterical and cries profusely, begging the social worker not to approach him for fear of him killing her.

The GP, warden, police, and neighbours all contact social services about Mr Smith (85), hit by a cyclist as he 'wandered' onto the main road. The GP confirms that his physical and mental condition has deteriorated: the police confirm that they have rescued him from a busy main road on numerous occasions, and the neighbours protest that this is only one example of Mr Smith's many bizarre and dangerous behaviours. All of these referrers demand that Mr Smith is admitted to an old peoples' home immediately.

The psychiatrist and GP request a section on a 40-year old divorcee, diagnosed as schizophrenic; she has been brought to their attention by increasingly anxious relatives and distressed neighbours. Both describe her hallucinatory, persecution-complex state, her moral and financial vulnerability to unscrupulous individuals, and the numerous hospitalisations previously. They both stress the urgency of the situation.

A gypsy family consisting of mother and seven children suddenly find father has gone and has taken caravan, truck and virtually every item the family possessed with him. The family have been referred round about midnight, by the police. They have been unable to find the husband. Mother and children are extremely distressed, tired, hungry and penniless.

Conclusion

Social workers will have no trouble in identifying such crises, and recalling numerous aspects of their own intervention attempts: the time at which they occurred, the place, the team and agency context, the supervision available, the impact of the crisis upon them, their thoughts and feelings, their initial reaction and approach, and indeed, the very question being asked here now: how relevant was all that crisis literature, much enjoyed on the course, to these typical crisis situations and the challenges they pose? Before answering, this social worker needs to reflect upon his own experiences and learning in crisis situations, beginning in the mayhem year of 1974. I would ask readers to tolerate the next chapter's largely subjective nature, but only because I am confident that it records an experience in which many can and still do share.

4

Reflections: a Crisis Learning Experience

Introductory lessons

Social workers can face the most unpredictable crisis situations for the most unusual reasons. During my very first social work visit, the father of the family approached me along the hallway with a rapidity of movement and a meanness in his eyes which betrayed his violent intent. He was big and strong and crude, and I held up my hand in a gesture of total submissiveness, and apologised if I was calling at an inconvenient time. I quickly retreated. Some time after, I met my predecessor for this particular case. He told me he had treated this family abominably-unintentionally of course. There was no explicit mention of this in the file, but a more careful reading revealed the sources of his admission, and clearly exposed the dangerously deteriorating relationship between them. The result was the client's almost pathological hatred of social workers and social services.

There were three important lessons in that experience. First, I learnt that I have quite a healthy instinct for survival and can easily tolerate a loss of faith and a dent in pride (much more preferable to a broken jaw!). Secondly, I experienced the prevalent nakedness of the social worker's situation in crisis: I was alone and frightened, many miles from the office, facing potentially violent strangers. Thirdly, the experience left the deepest and lasting impression of the self-provocative power of clients' perceptions of social workers and social services departments. In the years that followed, I was to learn of the significance of such perceptions when the social worker is attempting common crisis intervention tasks.

The agency context: post-Seebohm chaos

My colleagues were amused by this incident. We all had similar experiences to share. We would discuss them endlessly in open plan offices where some fifteen to twenty social workers, home help organisers, clerks, occupational therapists, etc., were supposed to work happily together, performing very differing tasks, demanding various degrees of intellectual effort and concentration. The crisis experiences fitted well into the general chaos. We did not really know what we were doing, where we were going, or how we were going to get there. Quiet rooms for honest reflections of one's unpleasant experiences, were frowned upon, and experienced, reliable, knowledgeable 'crisis' supervisors were non-existent – and still are, some may think. So the incidents were never analysed; the unpleasantness was merely ventilated and then forgotten about, until the next time, when one would be equally ill-prepared. The remedy in this case however, was quite simple: if I had known of the awful relationship between the clients and my predecessor – and that in itself may help one to avoid ugly scenes in the future – I could have written a letter stating my perplexity about the case, tactfully acknowledging the previous 'difficulty' in relationships and hoping they could enlighten me as to how it all came about. The worst and unlikely response would probably have been to tell me to naff off; but that would have been far more tolerable and a lot less serious than if I had to be carried off!

Divide and conquer

In my second involvement in a crisis, my lack of confidence and control in the situation compelled me to adopt a highly risk-laden, often counter-productive strategy. The child had undoubtedly been injured by the father, and not for the first time. It was mother who had made the frantic referral, alleging as much about wife battering as she did about child abuse at the hands of her husband. She wanted protection for both herself and her child, and she was not afraid to let her husband know that she was contacting social services.

It all seemed strange to me, particularly the fact that her husband knew. I most reluctantly went to investigate. But the nearer I got to the drab sixth-floor tenement flat in which they lived, the more discomforted and pre-occupied I was with this same fact: What was her reason for telling her husband? What would his reaction be? How tall was he? How violent? How hostile towards social workers? I was surprised and relieved to find him quite apprehensive towards me. He tried to appear relaxed and indifferent, even light-hearted for a time, but I knew he was genuinely worried. So was I. It was now obvious that the child battering was merely symptomatic of a complex game-playing family dynamics. I could easily sense it, but I did not understand it, and I had certainly no control over it. Mother repeated her allegations. Father denied, or claimed exaggeration, or made counter allegations. At times they were shouting at each other; then deadly silent; occasionally he tried to mock her, and all the time she would look in my direction, as if to say: 'Now you know what I'm up against.'

I could tolerate them 'performing' like this, but I could not tolerate my own impotence: an observer, a listener, making the occasional forced false and futile interjections. It was this feeling of powerlessness which made me suggest that I interviewed them separately. Mother was very keen; she had not been making much of an impression in the arguments. The father was less so, because beneath his half-humourous, mocking and unruffled manner, he really was worried about the consequences of this latest assault upon the child. Mother and I retreated to the kitchen. I immediately felt an enormous burden lifted from me. I actually had things to say then. She was grateful and gratified, continuing to project this image of herself and child living with a beast, and convinced now that I was on her side. Then it was the turn of her husband. I could see the distrust in his eyes as soon as he sat down. But it was surely nothing to what his wife began to feel, as a quarter of an hour later she burst into the kitchen, hurling abuse at both of us and claiming that I was being taken for a ride by a brutal, lying, thieving, adulterous bastard of a husband!

This was another unpleasant experience, yet in retrospect, there were signs of improvement. The relief I felt in separating them indicated how discomforted physically and emotionally I was. But within minutes of separating them, I experienced another kind of discomfort: conscience; it just did not seem right. As I listened to each of them, I felt myself sympathising more with the partner who was not there. I knew that they knew they were not being presented in a very favourable light. I imagined that, just as my conscience was applying more pressure on me, so too must the paranoia of the excluded partner have been intensifying. This was something of a dilemma, being reminded by conscience that I was doing wrong, and lacking the will and confidence to do right. But there were many similar dilemmas to follow; many temptations to adopt the same convenient but damaging strategy of separating the crisis participants, yet knowing not just the likely outcome, but the fact that such a strategy was primarily a symptom of my own weakness and incompetence. It is a difficult temptation to resist, not only because of the comfort and security it may offer in the midst of ugly, noisy, crisis situations, but because it is the traditional, standard way in which professionals of all kinds react to crises: doctors in their surgeries, police in their stations, headmasters and teachers in their schools; psychiatrists in their hospitals, and social workers in their offices are all capable of deluding themselves that their quiet and civilised chats with an individual miles away from the complex social and family circumstances in which the origin of that individuals' crisis lies, can contribute towards solving that crisis.

'Rescuing' clients from the crisis situation

It is of course very much in the professional's own interest to explore the crisis miles away from the crisis! But quite early in my career, I became aware of my projecting this need onto the client-particularly children at the centre of the crisis. I had this very powerful gut reaction towards children in cris is situations; it simply said: no child should be subjected to that particular physical or psychological abuse; no child should remain in that particular awful environment; worse that that, I had this near overwhelming urge to remove a child from such a situation, and place them in what I perceived as a haven of tranquility (quite rightly too) in which loving foster parents would fulfil their every need (very naive). This also applied even when the 'not so small' child had contributed to the crisis themselves, creating havoc in a residential home, stirring trouble between their natural and step-parent, assaulting a police officer and being temporarily locked up -the child had to be 'rescued' from all of this. But within days of the rescue, things started to go wrong. Foster parents could not cope; the child was becoming unmanageable; demands were being made to move them elsewhere. Whatever was happening?

The answer was quite simple in fact, and enshrines a crisis principle that has its origins as much in the natural sciences as in social work experience and practice.The crisis state is fundamentally one of processes; physical and mental processes which have required time and condition to reach the point of crisis. Irrespective of the pain and distress endured, some adaptation has taken place. To intervene and reduce the hostility and panic of a crisis situation, is certainly something that most of the crisis participants will welcome, and to which they will easily 'readapt'; but to remove a body from the crisis state, and place it in an environment totally unfamiliar in every respect, is in the long run certain to reap effects which are not likely to have been anticipated. Mother Nature within us, simply cannot cope with that lightning transformation, and is certain to kick out once she has got her breath back. Thus sixteen-year-old Valerie, having attacked residential members of staff and then locked herself in a room, threatening to commit suicide or murder anyone trying to stop her, was removed to a lock-up some twenty miles away; but no sooner was she there than she was 'rescued' by being removed to 'professional foster parents' another twenty miles away. Within a few days these professionals could not cope-through no fault of their own — and requested that Valerie be removed again. Another client, Simon, seventeen, whom I 'rescued' from an apparently brutal step-father, expressed the significance of this principle in a trance-like abstract way, nonetheless powerful in its effect on me. He was most withdrawn in the car as I drove him to the residential home; no matter which tactic I used, even silence itself, he would not respond; then, walking from the car he said: 'I can't believe this is real...I don't know what's happening to me'. He should have also said: 'This is most unnatural, and doomed to failure!'.

The redoubtable Erin Pizzey is thoroughly familiar with this principle. Nice middle-class social workers shriek in horror in their first visit to her battered wives' units. They are overcrowded, noisy, chaotic, even hostile; apart from safety, not all that much different from the environment the wives have left; and that is precisely as it should be. A much more recent and chilling example of this principle was provided in the Lebanese war. The doctor in the American hospital in Beirut must have shocked millions of viewers when he said that he and his staff dreaded the impact of a truce, particularly on their children patients. After months of daily bombardments throughout the town, the children greeted the first night of peace with uncontrollable panic and terror.

The agency: ally or foe?

The conflictual nature of crisis

What Caplan and his colleagues in those flower-power, liberating sixties did not realise was something that no social worker could fail to notice: crises are primarily about conflict — conflict between one individual and another, individual and family, individual and agency. It could be a conflict of interests, perceptions, loyalties, values or emotions, and any of these is capable of erupting in actual physical conflict. When a social worker is asked to intervene in a crisis, therefore, the question uppermost in the minds of the crisis participants will be: whose side is the social worker on? If a request or demand is being made to invoke statutory powers to 'solve' the crisis, the question is asked with greater urgency and apprehension. In a conflict situation, everyone needs an ally, and for many crisis participants there can be no stronger ally than the social worker called upon to solve the crisis.

Rapidly then, I was learning that crisis intervention can be a diplomatic nightmare, for which I was neither trained, experienced, nor competent. But neither was anyone else around me. I was confident enough about my learning capacities, and convinced I had the necessary sensitivity and compassion; but I most certainly had not yet acquired the ability to convey the impression of neutrality to all the crisis participants. Consequently I was playing the dual and opposing roles of ally and foe, occasionally generating the sense of triumphant vindication by the former, and hatred and fear by the latter, all of which feelings were guaranteed to make matters worse. During the years to follow, I gradually acquired some balance, enabling me to walk along this tightrope. It does not of course only apply to crisis; virtually all social work tasks require a nimble foot. But the urgency of crisis, the drama and high passion, the intense and unpredictable pressures demanding immediate responses – all these can make the tightrope that much slipperier, and the impact of the fall on either side greater. That fall can be made at the point of referral, long before the social worker gets to the crisis scene.

Crisis referrals

Inaccuracies, misunderstandings and dangers

Despite current opinion to the contrary, I was soon gaining an impression of social services as an organisation of unlimited patience and tolerance. This was most evident in the matter of referrals. It seemed that anyone could enter a social services office, speak to a duty officer, and get a crisis referral made either about themselves or someone else. Very little attention then was paid to a tiny box on the referral sheet, asking the social worker to tick 'yes' or 'no' as to whether the client was aware of the referral being made on their behalf. When I investigated the 'crisis' of old Mrs Collins, referred by a kindly neighbour who spoke of 'starvation' 'isolation'and 'odd behaviour', Mrs Collins not so kindly told me to clear off. When Mr Smith, the primary school headmaster – a much more respected referrer – pleaded for a social worker to intervene in the home situation of little Billy, who was describing how much his mother suffered at the hands of the stereotyped brutal step-father, I got myself immersed in long drawn-out, messy divorce proceedings, in which the only fact that could be established was that little Billy had a wonderful imagination, and relished the prospect of any audience ready to give him a hearing. When the district nurse referred the 'crisis' of old Winnie Arnott (96), living in one of the most isolated villages in North Yorkshire, she somehow forgot to add that Winnie was being cared for in the home of her daughter and son-in-law; that she also had two sons and their families living a few hundred yards away on their own separate farms; that in the next village two miles away there were two nieces and one nephew, and that all these family members between them made daily contact with Winnie, had never heard of social services, and had never dreamt of asking anyone for help, which of course is the principle reason why Winnie lived to the ripe old age of 96!

All of these cases were referred as crisis, which they most certainly were not. But they do illustrate the potential difficulties in which social workers can get embroiled, stemming from social services' open door policy directed towards any Tom Dick and Harry, and – sometimes worse – towards other professionals and agencies which have not the slightest clue about the functions of the department, nor indeed, have the ability to conceptualise their feelings and motivation beyond the core statement 'I think social services should be involved'. In the above examples, the consequences were not too serious: some irritation on the part of the clients, and a waste of valuable time and petrol by the social worker. But in the case of genuine crisis, I was beginning to find these casual, misinformed, hopelessly biased referrals potentially dangerous, particularly so if the referrer was also a crisis participant. They were dangerous not of themselves but because of the chain of events they initiated, beginning with the unavoidable fact that I, like every other social worker, was obliged to consider such referrals. In this mere act of consideration, sometimes involving the cosy and lengthy hospitality of our premises, and listening to those garrulous referrers with the most rigidly fixed notions of the origin of the crisis, its cause and consequences and what had to be done about it, I was in effect bestowing upon them a status and authority which had all sorts of implications for the crisis intervention task to follow. Again, I sensed this, and had niggling doubts about the ethics of the situation; yet I still firmly supported social services hospitality to anyone wanting to make a crisis referral. As the time of intervention grew nearer, my mind would concentrate wonderfully: how has the individual at the centre of the crisis reacted to the fact that a neighbour/friend/relative/GP/health visitor, has made a referral about them, and has divulged and discussed many intimate details of their private lives? More importantly, how would they react towards me? Would they perceive me as a dangerous authority figure who had been 'got at' by the referrer, one who had now 'taken sides' – an enemy to be resisted or fought to the bitter end? Such apprehensions were well-founded, because I did indeed encounter all kinds of covert and overt resistances, the former manifest in the client's refusal to speak to me, even to acknowledge my presense; and the latter in such hostile responses as: 'What have they been telling you?'; 'I didn't ask them to go to social services'; 'What right have you to be talking behind my back?'

It was quite some considerable time before I felt confident enough to avoid this particular pitfall. Today, I as tactfully as possible ask numerous questions of the referrer which they are not likely to have anticipated. And such questions are asked long before the referrer gets into an often comfortable and gratifying second gear: 'It's very kind of you to have taken the trouble, but before you tell me anything about this crisis, can I ask: Does Mrs Jones know you're here? What do you think she would say if she did? Does Mrs Jones want what you want? How do you think she's going to react to a social worker visiting? This crisis you talk about...it seems to involve the whole family...do you think I could talk to the family..?' No matter how tactfully and gently I learnt to ask such questions, they sometimes offended. But that was no bad thing, as long as the referrer was being made aware of the implications of their referral, and the fact that I was not going to side with them in any way against a prospective client.

Social services crises

But what kind of crises am I referring to? In the previous chapters I have implied a scepticism of the broad range of crisis situations chosen by all the prominent crisis pioneers to illustrate the crisis theories and models of intervention which they have propounded. That scepticism slowly evolved from my own crisis experience and from extensive readings of exclusively social work literature including the weekly social work journals. It was becoming increasingly evident that the vast majority of the crisis situations of the pioneering crisis literature were highly improbable in my daily experiences; improbable that is, in terms of the social class of the individuals in crisis, the nature of the crisis itself, and in my anticipated role and the statutory duties of the agency I represented. Here, for example are some specific categories of crises most familiar to me — for which there is precious little understanding and guidance in the literature: homelessness, absolute poverty, children left abandoned, children caught up in marital violence, juveniles creating havoc/assaulting residential workers/family mem-bers/police; fostering breakdowns, home placement break-downs, child battering, wife battering, and family crises arising out of the burdens of caring for the elderly, mentally ill and mentally and physically handicapped. Faced with any of these typical social services crises, I often found myself pondering on questions which the pioneers seemingly never had to ask:

1 . What impact(s) was the crisis having upon me?
2 . What impact(s) could my poor quality of intervention have upon the crisis processes?

3 .What are the resources of skill, knowledge, experience, etc., within social services, other agencies, and the community, needed to solve crises?
4 .How was I and the department perceived by the individual/family/community in crisis?
5 .What are the implications/consequences of such perceptions for the crisis intervention task?

The answers to these questions was not very reassuring. The first reply was that crises provoked a variety of feelings and responses in me: helplessness, fear, a sense of challenge, anger, irritation, confusion, excitement, enthusiasm and panic. Sometimes a mixture of such feelings constituted an unmanageable crisis within myself. The second reply was that my intervention could widen and deepen the crisis parameters. Third, that different crises demand different and entirely unrelated skills and resources to resolve them; fourth, that the crisis participants' perceptions of social services and the social worker ranged from utter indifference and ignorance to a paranoic fear and hostility, and fifth, such latter perceptions were a major obstacle to effective crisis intervention.

From these considerations emerged something of a conceptual framework, which, at the same time as it exposed my lack of crisis training, nevertheless was helpful in understanding the numerous complexities of the crisis situation and their impact upon me. In Table 4.1 the framework is applied to a number of very different crisis referrals.

Conclusion

Now let us return to those pioneers and their classical crisis literature. There is no disputing the fact that many of the principles which emerged from the work of the pioneers are as valid today as they were two and three decades ago – and such principles will be applied and acknowledged throughout this text. But it should also be recognised thet the substantial volume of literature which the pioneers produced, more specifically its 'form' 'content' and 'tone', is quite alien to most social workers' crisis experiences. In this literature,

Table 4.1 *The impact of different crises upon an inexperienced, untrained worker*

The Crisis	Impact on Social Worker	Resources Needed	Client's Perceptions	Implications/Consequences of Perceptions
Client, 22, male, diagnosed schizophrenic, is made to leave home by parents who cannot tolerate his behaviour. He gets lodgings, is robbed, takes heavy overdose, is hospitalised – in intensive care. Seen by psychiatrist, who decides not to admit. Client has been admitted numerous times previously. Social Services contacted by psychiatrist, then by parents. Parents very distressed, but are adamant they do not want son back again.	1. Feeling of frustration at not being involved earlier; a belief that social services are being used as dumping ground. (GP confides: 'Nothing can be done for him.') 2. Uncertainty as to whose crisis this is: the psychiatrist? GP? parents? hospital staff? social worker? or client? 3. The pervasive sense of being overwhelmed by a crisis of enormous dimensions and complexity.	1. Confidence and experience in mental health work and in consulting with medical personnel. 2. Assuring client of material and financial provision on discharge. 3. Ability to establish working relationship with parents, and explore origins of crisis. 4. Knowledge of, and contact with department's residential provisions for mentally ill. 5. A radically different approach to the failed medical-orientated treatment and responses to this particular client.	1. Before suicidal attempt, client's perceptions all despairing, because of chronic psychiatric illness, his parents rejection, the robbery in the lodgings, the attitude of his GP, his unemployment, poverty and homelessness. 2. After suicidal attempt, client is weak and exhausted, but welcomes social worker, and expresses gratitude. He perceives me differently from GP and parents, neither of whom have visited him in hospital. 3. Parents, particularly mother, perceives me as a threat, because I do not share the opinions and attitudes of medical personnel; because I am inquisitive about relationships within the family, and its history.	1. Client regards me as a last resort. I'm appalled by the attitude of medical personnel, yet I'm apprehensive of not doing any better; of being helpless if there is a further deterioration in his mental condition. 2. I feel strongly that client's problems should be explored in and with the family, but client and family are totally opposed to this, and only communicate with me separately. Their positions and attitudes are hopelessly rigid, and each tries hard to inculcate the same in me. 3. Mother ceaselessly attempts to justify her rejection of her son. She repeatedly chronicles the history of her own suffering caused by his mental illness.

The Crisis	Impact on Social Worker	Resources Needed	Client's Perceptions	Implications/Consequences of Perceptions
			4. Mother's strong feelings of guilt encourage her perceptions of me as biased, judgemental, and condemnatory.	4. I know well that my resistance to mother's attempts only reinforces her negative perceptions of me.
Three children, aged six, four and three, abandoned in police station after violent row between parents. Father walked out of home. Mother brought children to police station and then disappeared.	1. Initial surprise when detecting the anxiety of the police and their eagerness for me to remove children immediately. Police anxiety and pressure creates the same in me. I am more concerned about the children's needs.	1. Confidence, patience, experience and knowledge of area and locality where children live. Good community contacts to seek out parents/relations/neighbours/friends. Knowledge of and contact with fostering facilities in area. Contingency planning.	Two sets of clients: 1. The police 2. The children *Police perceptions*: they know I will solve 'their' crisis; they want me to do it immediately, which I cannot do. *Children's perceptions*: they 'understand' and feel safe with the police (who treat them with great kindness and hospitality). They do not understand 'social worker' or 'social services', and show no inclination to leave the police station.	1. Strong pressure from police nearly makes me do as they ask: remove the children without having done any preparation nor having a suitable alternative for them. Children's perceptions re-affirm my determination to leave them with the police until such preparations are complete.
Widower father of mentally handicapped client (18) dies suddenly. Neighbours/police want social	1. Anxiety 2. A sense of ignorance and helplessness.	1. Basic knowledge of mental handicap, and or knowledge of and contact with local mentally handicapped societies.	1. Client indicates his awareness of the significance of the event, but appears unable to comprehend the explosion of	1. Client's inability to verbalise impact of father's death contrasts sharply with the vociferous neighbours and police.

The Crisis	Impact on Social Worker	Resources Needed	Client's Perceptions	Implications/Consequences of Perceptions
services to 'do something'. Client is alone now.	3. Again, more conscious of, and receptive to pressures being applied by the neighbours and police, than the needs of client who cannot verbally express his feelings about the event.	2. Confidence/patience to explore with the help of those experienced in mentally handicapped, particularly medical personnel whether client can remain at home on his own (unthinkable to police and neighbours!)	concern; many individuals coming and going. Client's perceptions of social worker unknown.	The pressure they apply creates a lot of anxiety in me, and is a major obstacle to the lengthy processes of intervention which the crisis demands.
Cot death. Mother is known to the department, and is in a state of shock.	1. Confusion; apprehension; realisation of dichotomy of tasks and reluctance to attempt them: (a) bereavement counselling (b) explaining and participating in an elaborate and complicated administrative procedure involving police, medical personnel and coroner's office.	1. Expertise in bereavement counselling, specifically cot deaths. 2. Knowledge of administrative procedures involved. 3. Great sensitivity and tact to be able to carry cut these two very contrasting tasks simultaneously.	1. Parents see no role for social worker other than the offering of condolences. They perceive the GP as the principal source of help in this crisis, but make it clear that he has done nothing more than offer condolences himself. 2. Parents are baffled and annoyed by police involvement and the administrative procedures. They perceive these as 'heartless' and unnecessary.	1. I have no expertise or experience in bereavement counselling, either generally or specifically in cases of cot deaths. Yet even if I had, I sense that client's perceptions would make it difficult to find an entry point. 2. In explaining the administrative procedures going on all around them, I unwittingly encourage them to identify me as the cause of such procedures.

The Crisis	Impact on Social Worker	Resources Needed	Client's Perceptions	Implications/Consequences of Perceptions
Homelessness (a family from Scotland arriving in Selby, the husband hoping for work in the new Selby coalfield). The family have no money, nor food, and the wife and children are distressed.	1. This is a recurring crisis. The initial impact is one of irritation, knowing I am going to be with this family (three children) for some considerable time, and all other work sacrificed. But later, there is a more serious impact.	1. Determination/confidence. Consistency. Compassion. Above all, patience. This family has no roots in Selby; no sympathy therefore from housing department. I see my task is simply to provide them with food and persuade them to return to Scotland, with the provision of a travel warrant.	1. Family initially perceives social worker and department as agents that will somehow enable them to remain in Selby, find them accommodation. Such perceptions change drastically, and their feelings turn to outright aggression at one stage.	1. Pressure on the social worker to live up to their perceptions/expectations, and try to find them accommodation. When their perceptions change, pressure on the social workers to give way, and avoid the ugly, noisy, aggressive disturbances created by family.

crisis phenomena are observed and analysed, conceptualised and categorised in a strictly empiricist 'form' leading to the construction of all-embracing theories and models of intervention which never fail to solve any crisis. (Crisis literature lacks any descriptive accounts of failure, but then the sixties was not exactly an era for the expression of humility, and American psychiatrists have never been that way inclined!). Much of the 'content' of crisis literature, that is, the types of cases upon which the bulk of the literature and research is based and to which the intervention models are applied, is far from typical of the type of crisis situations referred to social services offices. And finally, the most significant characteristic, the style and 'tone' of classical crisis literature conveys nothing of the harsh realities of crisis intervention in social services: the atmophere of chaos, panic and fear; the acute poverty and appalling living conditions; the sprawling decaying council estates; the numerous crisis participants; the worker's uneasy awareness of the possibility of being overwhelmed by the crisis.

There is a crucially important area of social services crisis work in which all of these conditions abound. These are the PLEA-FOR-REMOVAL crises (O'Hagan, 1980a,b; 1984) which constitute the greatest single challenge facing social workers in British social services departments. These are the crises of greatest drama; the costliest crises in terms of suffering of clients, and of the emotional and financial expenditure on the part of worker and department respectively. The American psychiatric crisis pioneers knew nothing of these crises; knew nothing of the challenge they pose to the lone, crisis untrained, poorly supervised social worker, employed in chaotic, undisciplined, British social services departments; nor, above all, of the pressure brought to bear upon these same social workers, to invoke statutory powers to solve these crises. It is now time to explore the plea-for-removal crisis in depth, with particular attention given to the family and community context in which they erupt, and the social services context in which many expect and demand that they be resolved.

5

The Plea-for-Removal Crises

Definition

A plea-for-removal crisis is one in which family members,or neighbours, or relatives, or other professional agents and agencies, such as police, teachers, GPs, health visitors and district nurses, plead for, or urgently request the removal of the individual at the centre of the crisis. The following are examples of typical plea-for-removal crises most familiar to any social services office.

1. The mother and step-father of an 'unmanageable, defiant, destructive, glue-sniffing, fornicating, adolescent daughter' can take no more. They have tried 'loving' her, beating her, locking her out, depriving her of pocket money, and so on, but all to no avail. Now they believe their own relationship is in jeopardy: daily squabbles about their daughter, growing irritation with each other, mutual distrust and a sense of helplessness. The mother attacks her daughter with ferocity. She and her husband beg social services to take her into care.

2. The neighbours have said it; the health visitor has checked on it; the school and the GP confirmed it; and they all declare that nine-year-old Joseph and his eleven-year-old sister Marie, have been ill-treated, unfed, unwashed, and often ignored by their twenty-five year old single parent mother. They all contact social services and demand their removal, after Marie and Joseph have been knocking on neighbours' doors asking for money to buy food. Their mother is 'in town'.

3. Old Bill is eighty-five, senile, wandering in the dead hour of night, annoying his pensioner neighbours throughout the day, not eating well, leaving the heater and the gas on, and occasionally wetting himself. 'Take him away!' scream his neighbours; 'this man has got to go away,' say the police; 'he cannot possibly care for himself', says the GP; 'he'll drive us all batty!' cries the warden of the shcltered accommodation in which he lives.

4. The psychiatrist and GP seek compulsory admission of a forty-year-old divorcee, diagnosed as schizophrenic. She had been brought to their attention by anxious relatives and distressed neighours who have 'tried to help' and been hurt in the process. They describe her hallucinatory persecution-complex state, her moral and financial vulnerability to unscruplous individuals, and her numerous previous hospitalisations. They both stress the urgency of the situation.

The characteristics

There are a number of conspicuous features about crises like these. Firstly, the abnormal anxiety level of the crisis participants. Secondly, a request or plea is being made for action of the most drastic kind, the invocation of statutory power in pursuit of compulsory removal. Thirdly, the crisis participants, including other professionals, perceive social workers as enormously powerful people, the only people in fact, who can resolve these crises. And fourthly, the intensely conflictual nature of the crises. All these features combine to create a highly charged crisis atmosphere in which the clamour of friends, relatives, neighbours and professionals, can be overwhelming for the social worker and the department he represents.

Intervention: making the crisis worse

In the previous chapter, clients' and referrers' perceptions of social services were seen as an important factor in crisis situations generally. Much thought and care in how the worker responds is therefore necessary as this will undoubtedly play some part in effecting perceptions. But when a crisis situation deteriorates to plea-for-removal, the worker may not be afforded the opportunity to do anything about perceptions; they are likely to have been formed and entrenched quite some time ago. And they are usually the worst possible perceptions. Witness the distrust and fear-laden eyes of the mentally ill client who knows that the doctor or psychiatrist who has been attending them for months, has finally 'contacted' social services; or the terrified look in the eyes of the inarticulate teenage mother, clutching the baby she knows is the subject of gossip and innuendo which has finally reached the ears of the dreaded social worker now facing her. These clients are no longer interested in trying to turn the social worker into an 'ally' against the 'foe' of relatives and neighbours; they are now unshakeably convinced that the worker has already become the enemy, and should be treated accordingly.

In such situations, the worker's intervention initially intensifies the crisis. Social workers should not be unduly alarmed. Worsening the crisis or creating an entirely new but manageable crisis in order to tackle the original one is a well-established intervention technique adapted by for example, surgeons, politicians, and military strategists over many centuries. The difference of course may be that these professionals know what they are doing, in the sense that they intend to make the situation temporarily worse, and therefore expect it to get worse. The same cannot be said of social workers. Few social workers would admit that their arrival on the scene makes matters worse. More seriously, many social workers are not even aware that it does. This 'unawareness' and 'unintentionality' in respect of what actually happens – that is, the increase in tension and fear as the social worker steps into the plea-for-removal crisis arena – is a dangerous combination which does not bode well for the intervention to follow. If the worker is unaware, or does not accept that his initial contact worsens the crisis, then it is likely that he is also unaware of the therapeutic opportunities which such an impact affords: the principal one is that the focus shifts from the opposing sides of the crisis onto the worker himself. By acquiring the spotlight, the worker's prospect of imposing some degree of order upon the panic-stricken crisis situation is enhanced enormously. It will be demonstrated how later.

The shaping of perceptions

Why does a social worker's initial contact in a plea-for-removal crisis temporarily make that crisis situation worse? We can be certain of at least one reply.

Press and television has in recent years implanted in the minds of millions some very strange and unshakeable notions of what social workers do: for example, they take infants away from poor parents simply because they are poor; they take teenage children away when it is really that monster of a step-father who should be locked up; they are only a lackey of the psychiatrist doing the dirty work of signing people into asylums; they get the old folk put away into a workhouse. These are rather extreme examples of the media's portrayal of social workers. But they are the kind that stick, and they are quite likely to have played a significant part in the evolution of many real-life crisis situations. For clients generally, living in sprawling run-down council estates where much of social services efforts are concentrated, there is no shortage of evidence to reinforce these public perceptions of social workers. They should not be surprised therefore when their intervention heightens the plea-for-removal crisis and they hear statements like: 'It happened to Mary Williams...and it can happen here...': 'I told 'im a'd git the welfare if he did it again...'; 'We told 'er you'd take her away and lock 'er up...'; 'They need a lesson...and you're the one to give it...'.

These are in effect gross distortions about social work power and authority. They often stem from the inaccurate and damaging gossip in the surrounding community, from sensational past experiences in that same community, and, more potently perhaps than anywhere else, the mischievious imaginations of journalists, documentary producers, and dramatists, who are always interested in plea-for-removal crises, particularly if things go disastrously wrong. Alan

Bleasedale is one of many writers who recognise the dramatic potential in the plea-for-removal crises. He knows, perhaps better than most social workers, that their arrival on the crisis scene can initially heighten the tension and the danger. He exploited that to the full in his prize-winning 'Boys from the Blackstuff,' by creating a never-to-be-forgotten scene that symbolises so much of the public perceptions of social workers, and more importantly, the public's instinctive response to what social workers do. When Bleasedale's social workers with the help of an unbelievably sadistic group of police officers, remove the legendary Yosser's children, the camera zooms in on the 'teenage' middle-class posh-speaking worker who is naively trying to placate one of the hate-laden children she has removed. The child headbutts her for her troubles, and the nation laughs. More to the point, dangerous perceptions are reinforced, and social workers must be prepared for the hostility they generate in crisis situations. Otherwise, the initial worsening of the crisis may not be merely temporary.

The clamour for removal: the professionals

It can be seen now that there are four clearly-defined sources of pressure in these plea-for-removal crises.

1.   The crisis event and atmosphere generated;
2.   the clamour for removal by relatives neighbours friends and community;
3.   the requests or demands by other agencies;
4.   potential interest of the media and various pressure groups.

It may be suggested that a social worker should never have to face such formidable pressures alone, or indeed, never does, because of the back-up support of team, group leader, and the organisation (social services) generally. In the absence of research on the matter, I am convinced that individual social workers do face such pressures alone, and on those occasions when they do not, when they have all the built-in support of their department, the presence and involvement of group leaders and more senior management, such support may not be sufficient to withstand the clamour for removal.

A single parent mum who has two children, one asthmatic, and the other haemoephiliac, gives birth to a third, for whom there is a clamour for removal, chiefly from the GP, midwife and health visitor, on the grounds of the filth of the home, and the belief that the mother will not be able to cope. The social worker believes that these are not sufficient grounds for contemplating removal, nor does a paediatrician who has treated the two older children over a number of years, and has got to know the mother reasonably well. In an emergency case conference which includes divisional management representatives, and the present and former social workers, the decision is made to remove the baby, on the grounds that the filthy conditions create an unacceptable health hazard.

One may ask here how such a decision could be made in the light of opinion by such an eminent authority as the paediatrician, who clearly was against removal? The answer is simple: the influence of a paediatrician based in a hospital thirty miles away and coming into contact with the area office perhaps once in six months, is only a fraction of that exercised by the local GPs, health visitors, and midwives, who are in contact with our office virtually every day. And many of these colleague professionals – though they may not admit it – can be influenced and pressurised by numerous and persistent complaints by the neighbours. So too, can social workers.

The clamour for removal: the community

This is no shocking revelation, certainly no cause for ripples of guilt and inadequacy in social services departments. The fact is that much stronger and longer established institutions and professions have been giving way to such pressures for centuries. The most relevant example of such an institution is the 'asylum' and the profession, psychiatry. Langsley (1968b) Scott (1974) and Bott (1976) all describe the realities of these pressures which led to their analyses of the connections between prospective patients and their family/community environments: for instance, 'patients are not admitted out of a recognised desire to seek help...they are admitted to hospital through the demands of other people, usually relatives, and because the demands are rephrased as 'doctors orders', the hospital must inevitably act in the interests of the relatives and of society' (Bott, 1976, p.98).

It was this realisation that eventually led to the establishment of psychiatric crisis teams, of which Dr Scott's at the Napsbury hospital in Barnet is probably the best known. But such enterprises are few and far between; the vast majority of psychiatrists do not belong to any such teams, and remain as vulnerable to the considerable pressures exerted upon them. As Bott has pointed out, these pressures must increase for obvious reasons: the 'decreased density in the social networks of families and of individuals' (Bott, 1976, p.106). In other words, the break-up of whole communities, their scattering to those ghastly post-war desolate estates in which desertions and divorces have become rampant, have ensured that such communities do not have the strength, cohesion, and tolerance to be able to accommodate and defuse crisis situations to the extend they once did. 'The threshold of crisis has evidently been lowered' writes Bott (p.117), whose research showed that the number of mental illness crises and consequent hospital admissions had risen dramatically in the post-war decades.

Plea-for-removal: a 'dumping' crisis?

In the previous chapter, it was suggested that many crisis tasks fall exclusively within the boundaries of social services responsibilities. But this does not mean that significant others, lay persons and professionals from other agencies, are excluded from the course of events following the crisis. They may well be involved, and instrumental in helping the social worker resolve the crisis. The same cannot be said of many of the plea-for-removal crises. The plea itself represents the end of the road; the referral has been made to social services because only social services has the power (statutory) and the means (residential) to resolve the crisis in the way which referrers think it has to be resolved. These referrers are not interested in seeking help elsewhere. And when, as is often the case, the referrer happens to be a professional from another agency, the referral is usually being made on the basis of a sense of futility after many failed attempts to help the client. There is therefore a substantial 'dumping' aspect to the plea-for-removal crises. The health visitor, police sergent, GP and teacher are pleading on behalf of themselves as well as the client. They apply pressure to social services not just because the clients need help urgently, but also because of feelings of anxiety and guilt as a result of their not being able to provide that help themselves. Anxiety and guilt are probably the most common and easily projected feelings between one professional and another. And when unwary social workers absorb such feelings, they become far more vulnerable to the various other pressures which are being applied, by professional, relative, and neighbours alike. Pressures may also come from within one's own office. GPs, police sergeants, psychiatrists do not talk easily to mere social workers, particularly new and inexperienced ones. They are likely to make a concerted effort to enlist the support of management. Sometimes they may succeed. There is no more insidious device for undermining a social worker's confidence than the secret telephone conversations that seek to reverse their decision not to do a section; not to bring the child into care, or the elderly client into part III. None of this 'secrecy' nor 'dumping' of course, would be necessary if all crises were dealt with by multidisciplinary teams. But the vast majority of them are not, and the professional persons who make the plea-for-removal referral to social services usually want to have nothing more to do with the case, so frustrated have been their attempts to help in the past. This will be particularly so if the client/family are crisis-prone (Hill, 1965) and if various professionals have been involved simultaneously on previous occasions without any apparent success. Then the pressure applied to social services will be greater, based though it is on the non-professional, emotive expressions of exasperation, like: 'Everything's been tried... there's nothing more can be done'.

Plea-for-removal: unrecognised suffering and care

It is easy to project the client at the centre of the plea-for-removal crisis as a victim encircled by individuals who do not understand, who lack compassion and sensitivity, and who all clamour for the client's removal for their own selfish reasons. This is a nonsense cultivated by numerous social work writers in the sixties in particular. Any attempt to instil some reality into this scenario must begin from a much broader perspective that enables the viewer both to see and to understand the complex historical and present interpersonal dynamics between client and family/community/environment. Families and communities are not normally bent on getting members removed and locked up. Their tolerance level may well have been lowered as Bott (1976) implies, by urban social and demographic forces over which they may have no control, but they still display enormous resources of adaptation and resilience faced with numerous provocations in their daily lives. The high stakes mentioned in regard to the client at the centre of the plea-for-removal crisis, apply equally to the family and community. If the client (justifiably) sees their home, children, liberty or sanity at risk by the threat of removal, so too may the family/community justifiably see precisely the same by the threat of the client remaining. Reality in this respect certainly has come to the fore in literature pertaining to the crisis of psychiatric hospital admissions. Whereas Goffman (1961), portrayed the psychiatric patient as one upon whom every conceivable indignity was inflicted by every single member of staff in the institution, thereby ensuring that they would remain incarcerated, Bott devotes considerable space to the sufferings and fears inflicted upon the family by their mentally ill member.

The person (client) behaves in a way that destroys the sense of self of the people close to him. He wrecks havoc in their feeling that their world is as it used to be and ought to be...The view that madness is only deviance from conventional norms fails to appreciate the destruction the mad person, or more accurately, the mad part of the person, wrecks not only on conventional society but on any form of society. The view that the patient is an innocent victim ignores or fails to see the extent to which he controls and manipulates both his associates and himself to destroy the basis of thinking and gratification both for himself and for them. (Bott, 1976, p.118)

This kind of eminently sensible redress will ring true in the minds of experienced social workers. Few of us have escaped the dangerous indoctrination which Bott refers to, which allowed us in the early stages of our careers to respond to the psychiatric emergency with more idealism than sense. There is a need for a similar reawakening in other plea-for-removal spheres more familiar to social workers, for instance, the unmanageable adolescent living with step-parent(s); the confused elderly person living alone. Again one must begin by dispelling the myth which may have its origins in training, social work publications, or in the minds of prize-winning dramatists, the myth that every teenager and elderly person at the centre of the crisis is a victim being hounded out of their homes by stupid intolerant and cruel people. This myth should be dispelled easily by a fact and a faith essential in social work. First, the fact which Barclay (1982) acknowledged: that ordinary families and communities provide of their own volition all but a tiny fraction of care for the various client groups in their midst, and particularly for the elderly. Social workers are well placed to confirm this. Secondly, social work is to some extent an act of faith which must emphasise the humanity of all citizens (Davies, 1981, p.37) irrespective of the situation in which the worker finds himself. It is easier said than done. If the bruised adolescent weeps and the angry muscular step father hurls abuse at the social worker demanding that the child be removed, it is extremely difficult to concentrate the mind on the assailant's 'humanity'. But a useful starting point is that the plea-for-removal is also a plea to 'prevent me from injuring my step-child any further'. Step-parents can inflict great suffering upon their step-children. But when a social worker investigates the genesis of the plea-for-removal crisis, they will discover a complex web of intrigue, game-playing, alliances, and diversions, in which all family members have suffered and lost, and – in this writer's experience – the step-parent may well have lost most. Few step-parents accept the responsibility of someone else's children without the intention and the hope of providing for them well. When all is not well the last thing they need is an intervention that gives official recognition to the centuries-old myth about step-parents.

In the case of referrals pleading for the removal of the elderly confused person, it is even more important for social workers to exercise this faith, by examining carefully the nature of the clamour by the client's relatives, and/or neighbours. These people do not simply waken up some day and decide that old Mrs Wilkins has got to go. Their plea is more likely to be a dreaded climax to years of sacrifice of time, effort and expense on behalf of Mrs Wilkins. And the referral is usually made after a series of incidents which demonstrate that the client is incapable of remaining alone without a level of risk which they regard as frightening, for themselves as much as for the client.

There are other more powerful motivating factors which social workers have to be aware of. First, as in all plea-for-removal referrals, there is a major anxiety-inducing ingredient which may be accurately described as the 'What if something terrible happens?' syndrome (O'Hagan, 1980b). It is not just the increasing fear of the child being battered to death, nor of the mentally ill person taking their own life or somebody else's, nor of the elderly resident in their midst suffering the terribly lonely protracted death after a fall when nobody was about; a more potent source of their fear and anxiety is what will society at large think of them if such tragedies do occur. Ironically, it is the social work-bashing press they fear most of all, imagining the biggest and blackest headlines denouncing 'the community that didn't know nor care'. For an elderly community – and it is nearly always the elderly who care for their own – such a scenario can give rise to individual and collective paranoia far more challenging than anything envisaged in the original referral.

The second major source of fear and anxiety is, quite frankly, a 'taboo' topic which must not be discussed at the time of the crisis referral. To be daily confronted by the inevitable decay in the human condition: the drift into senility and all its consequences in the physical and psychological condition of the client, the apparent loss of dignity and self-respect, the end of self-determination, and, worse still, the image that all of this is one's own fate, is often too much for a community of elderly helpers to bear, particularly if they have made strenuous efforts on behalf of the client, to delay these inevitable processes. They will want that client removed not just because she poses an unacceptable high risk to her own life and the lives of the people nearest her, but also because her worsening condition actually confirms in their own minds that they themselves are becoming too old, feeble and intolerant to be able to do anything about it.

Plea-for-removal: the diminishing options

It is now obvious that the social, environmental and psychological dimensions of the plea-for-removal crises are virtually unlimited. In this writer's experiences these types of crisis have increased dramatically during the last decade, and there are reasons to believe that their numbers will continue to rise, nationwide. As social services departments become longer established and better known, so too will more citizens refer crises to them. The number of elderly people continues to rise sharply, and as the NHS and social services are forced to make cuts in the provision of services for them, it is likely that there will be a corresponding increase in the number of plea-for-removal referrals made ostensibly on their behalf. The intensification of poverty and deprivation caused by the massive increase in unemployment, and a similarly alarming increase in the number of reconstituted families as a consequence of the staggering divorce rate, will both inevitably bring many more families to the brink of crisis; the crisis of child abuse, mental illness, teenage/step-parent conflict. In the eyes of many of the crisis participants, including professionals from other agencies, these crisis can be solved only by the removal of the individual at the centre of them. But ironically such trends and such perceptions coincide with a policy aimed at the drastic reduction of the very residential establishments in which the hopes of those clamouring for removal is vested. Which means that the social worker will often have to face a plea-for-removal crisis knowing that whatever he finds, his residential options have been slowly ebbing away during the past few years, and indeed, for certain client groups, may now be non-existent, or at least entirely inadequate.

Plea-for-removal crises then, constitute the most complex and demanding challenges for both social worker and social services departments. For the former, there is

(a) the drama and passions in the crisis event itself;
(b) the chaos of such a large number of crisis participants, usually family members who are involved,
(c) the prospect of invoking statutory powers to remove someone;
(d) the pressure applied by other agencies; and
(e) the possible isolation of the lone social worker perhaps miles away from the comradeship of their office base.

These are enormous burdens and responsibilities which the social worker carries on the department's behalf. The danger is that social workers, untrained and inexperienced in crisis work, unskilled and inadequately supervised, can be easily overwhelmed by such a crisis event, and attempt to escape by the quickest possible means. Thus the fear of crisis situations becomes internalised, only to become manifest even more strongly during the next similar crisis challenge. The 'quickest possible means' referred to here, is obviously a removal of the client at the centre of the crisis, and if there is, as suggested, a dearth of residential options, the placement is likely to be wholly unsatisfactory, doing little for the client or the immediate family, and least of all for the social worker's confidence and morale. For the department, there is the prospect of a perpetuation of its reputation as portrayed by the media: baby-snatcher, gaoler, the dictatorial, impersonal, insensitive bureaucracy with far too much power over the lives of ordinary citizens; and there is the reality of the department becoming embroiled in a messy, protracted and very expensive statutory obligation for which the provision of long-term care is the most conspicuous feature. The unfortunate thing about responding to the plea-for-removal crisis by actually removing, is that it becomes the precedent for all involved, particularly for the family, and any future attempt to respond differently will incur the stiffest opposition.

Conclusion

It is now time to turn away from the state of crisis intervention today, and to explore the ways and means of responding more effectively to crises in the future, particularly those in which a plea-for-removal is being made. The knowledge-base of crisis intervention, its theory, practice, context and literature has been examined and seen to be wanting in the context of British social services departments and the crisis tasks faced by social workers employed by them. Of the many flaws in that knowledge-base, the most important and dangerous is the total ignorance of the significance and power of clients' and referrers' perceptions of social workers and social services departments. Any alternative crisis intervention knowledge-base will need to stress this factor. It will also have to produce a literature of theory and practice relevent to the realities of social work practice in Britain today. The principles, skills, and techniques which it espouses and teaches, will have to be formulated around lone social workers facing crises in dilapidated homes and estates, in the midst of dismembered families and participating neighbours, relatives and friends. Above all, this new knowledge-base needs to stress the necessity of a high level of self-awareness on the part of the worker; an awareness of one's own standards of knowledge, experience, skill and competence in crises; more importantly, an awareness of one's own vulnerabilities in the crisis situation, the initial impact of that vulnerability, and its influence throughout the intervention.

Within that new knowledge-base lies the exciting prospect of two kinds of confidence that will enable workers to deal far more effectively with typical social services crisis situations. The first is the confidence naturally derived from knowledge itself. But the second is the rarer, quieter and more precious confidence derived from honesty and humility. Both are attainable.

6

A New Foundation For Crisis Training

Introduction

This chapter will attempt to lay a theoretical foundation on which to build a crisis training programme. It will advocate the use of an already established discipline, offering a relevant knowledge-base and literature, and principles and techniques which can be seen to work in crisis situations faced by lone social workers in deprived communities and dismembered families. A theory of crisis is needed which will be particularly suited to this social services crisis context; which will accentuate the conflictual nature of crisis situations, and enable the worker to gain a mental grasp of the usually large family and social dimensions of crisis. Theory is also necessary to elicit form and meaning out of the chaos and panic which threatens to engulf workers in crisis situations. The chapter will then concentrate on two areas of crisis intervention which are of crucial significance: clients' perceptions of social services in a crisis situation, and the necessity of social workers being fully aware of their own vulnerabilities in crisis work. A conceptual framework is provided to enable social workers to explore their vulnerabilities in various crisis contexts.

Family therapy

The crisis situations which social workers have to face nearly always involve the individual client's immediate family, and sometimes other relatives, friends and neighbours. Clearly then, the psychoanalytic orientation of traditional casework and classical crisis literature is unsuitable as a base for establishing crisis intervention practice in social services departments. Langsley *et al.*(1968a) pointed the way to a new approach when he commented at the end of his own crisis research: 'those who investigate crises should look at the family setting in which they arise' (p.155). Fortunately social workers have no option but to look at the family setting, as they will more often than not be dealing with the crisis in the client's own home, and most likely be facing a barrage of conflicting interpretations from family members as to what the crisis is all about. Since Langsley made that comment, family therapy has emerged as the principal means by which welfare professionals can explore the family context of a client in crisis, and attempt to engage family members in helping to solve the crisis. Family therapy views the family as the most influential context in which crisis occurs. Family therapists believe that families have 'the greatest impact upon the production, maintainence and resolution of a particular crisis' (Umana *et al.*, 1980, p.6). From the outset, family therapists insist on assessing by conducting whole family interviews; then the strategies they devise necessitate whole family participation. It is this preoccupation with the whole family, their opinions and prejudices, their relationships with each other, their alliances and divisions, their fears and hopes, their strengths and weaknesses, and the impact of all these upon the individual client in their midst and the problem they present, which makes family therapy an appropriate diagnostic and intervention tool for social workers facing the type of family pressures already discussed. Family therapy is most sensitive to two of the risk factors to emerge out of that discussion; it emphasises

(a) the danger of focusing upon and possibly exposing any one individual at the centre of the crisis; and

(b) the pitfall of allying oneself with the referrer or any group against the client.

Common goals in family therapy and crisis intervention

The 'therapeutic potential' of family crisis situations is a principle well-recognised by social workers and family therapists alike. Families enduring the distress and panic of crisis situations, are far more receptive to intervention than they normally are. The worker therefore has greater opportunity to break through the rigidity of entrenched and destructive behavioural and relational problems which are often the root cause of the crisis. This principle first assumed significance in the work of Caplan (1961), but it is in fact a conviction from a much older social casework practice, given the social work clarity and status it deserved by Rapoport (1971) and stumbled upon in a roundabout way by family therapy pioneers, notably Jackson (1957) and Minuchin and Fishman, (1981). As Hoffman (1971) observed, the principle was: 'what Jackson and other family therapists realised when they tried unsuccessfully to introduce changes into families which were not in crisis...' (p.292). A little note of caution should be struck here. As will be demonstrated later, the 'therapeutic potential' of crisis situations in the social services context may be extremely limited.

Another principle turned-goal adopted by the family therapists and ideal for crisis intervention in social services, is that the right kind of minimal intervention during a crisis can achieve a maximum and optimum effect. Social work clients and their families, many of them poverty-stricken, disorganised, and dismembered, neither want nor are able to respond to the traditional long-term, systematic, mutually planned treatment programmes. Their burdens and deprivations can be such as to drastically limit their ambitions and organisational capacities to something as basic as daily survival without some additional catastrophe befalling them (O'Hagan, 1983b). Such clients are action orientated when they experience a crisis. They want immediate and visible results, which is precisely what a social worker should strive to achieve.

There is one further point to be made in advocating family therapy. Classical crisis literature has been criticised because its form, content and tone reveal nothing of the atmosphere of crisis situations, nor of the complexities and dangers of the crisis task. Invariably and predictably, it demonstrates only success. Family therapy literature however, also vividly describes failure, and analyses the causes of it. It explores the obstacles and resistance of the family; it concentrates on the therapists' vulnerabilities and how these adversely affect the quality of the intervention; overall, it provides a comprehensive view and insight into the impact the therapist has made upon the family and vice versa. Family therapy literature expresses a humility and honesty which is extremely rare in the writings of the professional classes. It is its emphasis upon 'self' and 'self-awareness' which constitute a major new lesson for social workers, and which makes a vital contribution towards individual competence in crisis situations.

Towards a new theory of crisis for social workers

Family therapy theories

Social workers may be excused a certain degree of scepticism towards the bewildering array of theories in evidence in family therapy literature. The family therapy tree has many branches now: the psychoanalytic (Boszormenji-Nagy and Framo, 1965; Cooklin, 1979); behaviourist (Eisler and Hersen, 1973; Douglas, 1980); communications (Watzlawick *et al.*, 1966); psychodynamic (Ackerman, 1966); structural (Minuchin, 1974); strategic (Cade, 1980; Maldanes, 1980); systems (Walrond-Skinner, 1976); paradox (Palazzoli *et al.*, 1978). And in addition there is also a branch of influential anti-theorists, headed by Whitaker (1973). Nevertheless, it is essential for social workers engaged in family crisis work to have some theoretical basis underpinning their perceptions of the crisis event. And before choosing a theoretical base it is useful to reemphasise the context and challenges of crisis work in social services.

1.   Social workers in social services departments rarely work with the 'nuclear' complete family which is the standard model upon which so many theories of families

are based. They are more likely to be working with step-parent,cohabittee families; and quite often with two and three-family families, none of which bear any resemblance to the original nuclear family units. Many of them are afflicted in varying degrees with grinding poverty, unemployment, criminal records, and stigma, and are crisis-prone (Hill, 1958).

2. Such families can be influenced considerably by friends, neighbours, relatives and other agencies, some of whom are likely to be involved at a time of crisis.

3. Social workers are often under pressure to invoke statutory powers to remove the client at the centre of the crisis. This pressure may be applied by family, neighbours or other agencies.

4. Social workers intervening are likely to have a powerful impact upon the crisis, irrespective of their degree of competence. Their thoughts, feelings, perceptions, utterances and actions can all influence the crisis processes.

5. Social workers often have to face crisis situations alone.

Despite the scope of this unique context and challenge, there is no need for the family therapy tree to give birth to another theoretical branch solely in the service of crisis social workers. (And one cannot help thinking that if some zealots insist on squeezing another branch from it the poor thing will surely strangulate, collapsing into another pseudo-therapeutic heap!). There are a number of reasons for choosing systems theory to provide the theoretical base for family crisis work in social services departments. First, it is already a familiar theoretical base in social work education (Davies, 1977; Forder, 1976; Goldstein, 1973; Janchill, 1969; Vickery, 1974). Secondly, some of its key concepts dominated (and were occasionally misused in) the earlier theories of crisis and the models of crisis intervention. Thirdly, as family therapy is regarded as the major influence on family crisis intervention, it is reassuring to know that systems theory is family therapy's most enduring, flexible and expansive theoretical base (Walrond-Skinner, 1984). Even Minuchin's popular 'structural' family therapy borrows heavily from systems concepts when dealing with family crises (Minuchin *et al.*, 1981), and a much more rigourous examination of family crisis phenomena by family therapists relying on systems theory is provided by Hoffman (1971). Finally, it is this flexible and expansive nature of systems theory which enables one to apply it in seeking to understand, and to formulate strategies for working with, those dismembered poverty stricken families who are so far removed from their original nuclear family units, and who are totally enmeshed with similar groups all around them. Indeed, because of the degree of dismemberment and enmeshment, 'social system' maybe a far more appropriate term than 'family' and systems theory is particularly valuable in understanding the relatedness of social systems (Forder, 1976).

It falls far beyond the scope of this text to provide a comprehensive survey of systems theory. Many of the writers above have already done so, and the two chapters on systems theory in Davies (1977) are to be specially recommended. However, some of these writers explain systems theory in terms of the widest possible application, adorning it with an omnipotence and jargon that has provoked Jordan (1977) into ridicule:

> The unitary approach (systems theory) reconciles every opposite, slackens every tension, soothes every passion, and replaces the will to get involved (at any level) with a tidy diagram. My own experience of trying to talk to a group of students reared on a diet of systems theory is that they smilingly translate everything said to them, however angrily, bitterly, or ironically, into their own obscure jargon, repeating it back indulgently to the uninitiated. (p.450)

Jordan's pungency would be delightful were it not indicative of the anti-theory backlash to the admittedly endless stream of social work theories of the sixties and seventies. But his criticism is also partly based on a rather superficial grasp of the theory, a preoccupation with the sight and sound of systems jargon. Jordan and many others may be excused for this; social work writers on systems theory invariably got bogged down with explanations of purely technical aspects of systems. Similarly, their illustrative diagrams resemble technical drawings rather than human or social systems. The emphasis is on the mechanics of systems rather than on their vibrant varying processes, the processes of 'growth' and 'change' for example, upon which systems theory, more than any other in social work literature, concentrates.

Deriving a theory of crisis from systems theory

The crisis system

In social work, the processes of a particular crisis event can be viewed as an unique social system, in which probable sources of influence such as the referred client, social worker, police, GP, health visitor, friends, neighbours, relatives, and so on, represent interconnected component parts, which may be called subsystems. Surrounding the crisis system are the neighbourhood and community which may be referred to as supra-systems. A central tenet of systems theory is particularly true of crisis situations: 'all systems but the largest are themselves subsystems of other systems, and all systems but the smallest are environments for other systems' (Forder, 1976, p.26). In a family or social system in crisis, the referred client is perceived by many to be at the centre of the crisis, both its cause and principal effect, but within the system's perspective, he or she is merely a component part of a whole system, and not necessarily either the most important or affected part. A system in crisis may have undergone such fundamental change in its basic structure, its divisions of power and goals, and in its level of function and dysfunction, that it is totally unrecognisable from its previous healthy state. 'I don't know how it could have come to this...'; 'I'd never have believed we could do this to each other...'; 'Whatever's happened?....; It was never like this before...'.; these common utterances from crisis participants indicate that even they, as the central protagonists in the drama, recognise that their once tolerable family/social system has collapsed, and that the dominant characteristics of the crisis system replacing it are chaos and wholesale dysfunction, meaning acute suffering and distress for those involved.

Closed and unhealthy 'open' systems

An important aspect of the social work task in crisis situations is encapsulated in systems theory's concept of 'open' and 'closed' systems:

> Organic systems (i.e., either social or biological) are 'open', meaning they exchange materials, energies or information with their environments. A system is 'closed' if there is no import or export in any of its forms, such as information, heat, physical materials, etc., and therefore no change of components. (Hall and Fagen, 1956, p.23)

There is an obvious implication here that 'open' systems are healthy and 'closed' systems unhealthy. Generally, this is true; as individuals and families, we cannot afford to be cut off from the community, work force, and society in which we live. But a system in crisis may be different. The crisis may indeed be intensified by too much input from the outside world. Many dismembered poverty-stricken families in crisis open their doors to anyone in the vicinity. There is seldom a shortage of local 'counsellors' 'advisors' and 'supporters' eager to accept the invitation. Whilst this may temporarily alleviate some of the crisis participants, it can create enormous problems for the social worker. Where are the boundaries of this crisis system? is, for example, a likely and urgent question, if one is confronted by a ceaseless barrage of interpretations allegedly supported or contradicted by Mrs Smith next door, Mr Jones across the street, the headteacher, the shopowner at the corner, the remaining family members, or even a distant relative. It may take a while and a good deal of experience for social workers to acknowledge that

(a) any one of these subsystems may be the most dysfunctional and therefore the most damaging within the overall crisis system;

(b) if that is the case, then it may be necessary for the social worker to redraw the crisis boundaries, diminishing them to manageable proportions, and excluding any subsystem which is blatantly unhelpful.

Pittman *et al.* (1971) argues for the exclusion of the 'peripheral flame thrower', someone whose role has become important as a reaction to the crisis; for example, a relative or neighbour who is trying to 'help' but in reality is only 'keeping the
crisis going' (p.263). This tightening of the boundaries and
exclusion of such individuals need not be a monumental task.
It will be demonstrated in a later chapter that it can easily be
done by a combination of honesty, directness and humour.

Struggle and conflict in crisis

Morphostasis and morphogensis

Struggle and conflict are characteristic of many crisis situations, for instance, the married children of an elderly person
at risk, arguing and fighting about who is or should be
responsible for that elderly person's safety and welfare; the
strict religious parents fighting to maintain moral authority
over a wayward adolescent; a battered wife or child; frequent
conflict with a mentally ill client in one's midst; and the
numerous crisis struggles and conflict between clients and
agencies like DHSS, police, housing department, and so on.
It can be seen that many of these conflicts stem from
incompatible goals. Living systems are goal-orientated.
Systems theory emphasises that subsystems within a system
may have different goals from one another and from the
system as a whole. Human social systems are also value
orientated. Similarly, therefore, conflict may stem from
opposing values.

There are two opposing processes in any living system:
'Morphostasis' and 'morphogenesis'. Morphostasis is
associated with the status quo, structure, pattern, regularity
and constraint. 'It is essentially concerned with the
preservation of what is' (Walrond-Skinner, 1976, p.14).
Morphogenesis is associated with change, differentiation,
innovation, and creativity. It helps the system's component
parts to develop in their complexity and individuality. It is
entirely wrong to regard morphostasis as dysfunction, and
morphogenesis as always desirable. The health of a system
depends upon some degree of the structure and constraint
associated with morphostasis, and upon some degree of the

change, growth and differentiation associated with morphogenesis. These two opposing processes of morphostasis and morphogenesis generate a certain degree of tension. This is vitally important for the health and development of the system. There can of course be too much tension or too little, caused by the dominance of either process. A system in which the morphogenic processes are rampant and the morphostatic processes are inoperative is one which is in a state of permanent revolution. A system in which the morphostatic processes dominate to the extent of excluding all morphogenic processes is one which is in a state of decay. The normal healthy condition of living systems depends upon the simultaneous operation of both opposing processes, and the generation of a minimal degree of tension between them. A 'steady state' is maintained in such systems, allowing for normal growth and change.

The morphostatic and morphogenic processes operate within a safe boundary called 'homeostasis'. But whereas the morphostatic processes are easily accommodated within that boundary and serve to protect it, the morphogenic processes are constantly striving to move (deviate) beyond it.

Each system has an inbuilt monitoring and interpretative mechanism called feedback. The time-honoured example of feedback, in all systems literature, is that of the thermostat. When the temperature rises to a point beyond which there is risk or danger, the thermostat switches off the supply. When the temperature falls below a certain (safe) point, it switches on the supply. There are two types of feedback within systems, negative and positive. Negative feedback (as in the thermostat) counteracts deviation. Positive feedback encourages it. Negative feedback serves the morphostatic processes, whilst positive feedback serves the morphogenic processes. The value of either type of feedback depends entirely upon the circumstances in which it is activated, and the consequences of that activation on the systems as a whole. Often, both mechanisms will be activated alternately, reacting to the situation brought about by each. The common family bickerings and rows provide an example of this. The vast majority of these peter out with no lasting damage done. But if they increase in frequency and duration, particularly around some acutely sensitive family issue, then there is a danger of either positive or negative feedback seeking a runaway victory at the expense of the other. If the morphostatic processes and the negative feedback which serves them triumphs in a runaway sequence then the homeostatic boundary will be strengthened, and the system will become far more resistant to necessary growth and change. If the morphogenic processes and the positive feedback which serves them triumph in a runaway sequence, then the homeostatic boundary will collapse, and the system's component parts will break out of all homeostatic constraints (that is, conformity, values, structure and so on). In either of these extremes, the system's 'steady state' with all its necessary 'minimal tension', will cease to exist.

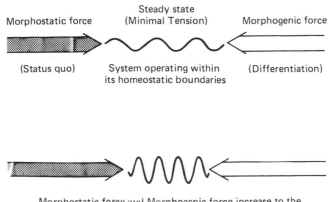

Figure 6.1 *Mophostasis and morphogensis*

The point should be made that the crisis pioneers used systems terminology rather loosely and inaccurately; so too, have many social work and family therapy writers. The most ill-used term is 'equilibrium', assumed to mean something desirable, like a balanced state. In systems theory however, the meaning is precisely the opposite; it is a state of no growth or change, a state of standing still – which in fact is the dictionary meaning of the word – or, as the most prominent systems writer, Bertalanffy (1968) puts it: a state of decay. The following diagram illustrates concepts we have been discussing in their most basic and simple form.

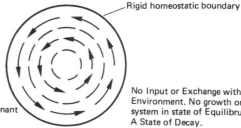

Rigid homeostatic boundary

Morphostatic forces
(Status Quo) totally dominant
within system.

No Input or Exchange with
Environment. No growth or change
system in state of Equilibrum i.e.
A State of Decay.

Figure 6.2   *Morphostatic 'victory'*

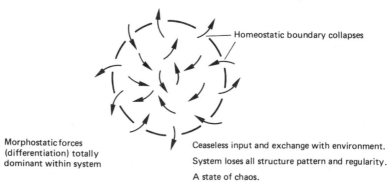

Homeostatic boundary collapses

Morphostatic forces
(differentiation) totally
dominant within system

Ceaseless input and exchange with environment.

System loses all structure pattern and regularity.

A state of chaos.

Figure 6.3   *Morphogenic 'victory'*

The application of the theory

Let us now look at an actual plea-for-removal case within the framework of these systems concepts and the theory derived from it. Typically, this crisis is characterised by chaos, panic, numerous participants, and a clamour for removal.

Mr Black (78) lodges in the home of Mrs Smith (80). Previously he lodged in the home of Mrs Smith's daughter Mrs Jay, next door. She is a single parent with three children Pauline (19), Gary (17), and Ann (13). Previous to that, he lodged with Mr and Mrs Hammond, who live a few doors away in the same terrace block of council homes. Mr and Mrs Hammond could not cope with Mr Black. They asked him to leave. Mrs Jay took him in, but soon realised that she could not cope either, and ordered him to leave. Her mother, Mrs Smith, living next door, offered to take him. The frantic telephone call comes from Mrs Smith's daughter, Mrs Jay. She said that her mother is being 'driven to distraction' by Mr Black. He is drinking constantly and making a general nuisance of himself, 'just like he did when he was here, and in Mr and Mrs Hammonds'. Mrs Jay has just had an 'almighty row' with Mr Black. She saw him returning drunk to her mother once again, and went to confront him. During the row, Mr Black accidentally broke an expensive and sentimentally valuable piece of china. He ended up threatening Mrs Jay. She is convinced he is 'mental' and she is afraid of him doing harm to her mother. Mrs Jay rings the office and begs the department to get Mr Black out 'before something terrible happens'.

Although Mrs Jay can hardly be seen as an objective observer, let us assume for the moment that her referral is reasonably accurate, in order to approach this crisis through a systems perspective. It is in many ways a typical morphostatic/morphogenic conflict situation, which indeed, would have been entirely predictable had the theory been applied long before any of the crisis points had been reached. Mr Black is a wandering destitute finding it difficult if not impossible to settle down and conform to some degree of regularity and constraint. The family systems of the Hammonds, the Jays, and Mrs Smith, are largely morphostatic in operation; they depend upon much regularity, predictability, and domestic routine. These established family systems cannot cope with the alien subsystem of Mr Black. Two of them (the Hammonds and the Jays) have got rid of him after obvious rising tensions, conflict, and crises. Now the same is threatening in the home of Mrs Smith, no doubt influenced by what has happened in the homes of the Hammonds and the Jays. It is also reasonable to suggest here that none of these systems have an effective monitoring or feedback mechanism (such families are likely to be far more compassionate than they are wary or sophisticated). Consequently, the predictable warning signals about Mr Black's behaviour and his difficulty in conforming have either been unseen or ignored. The inevitable rising morphostatic/morphogenic conflict in each of the systems can be represented as in Figure 6.4.

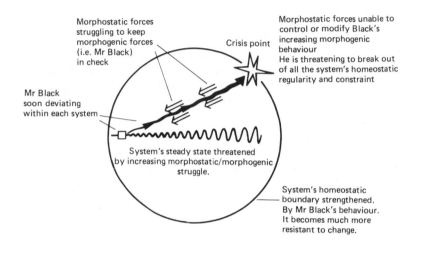

Morphostatic forces struggling to keep morphogenic forces (i.e. Mr Black) in check

Crisis point

Morphostatic forces unable to control or modify Black's increasing morphogenic behaviour
He is threatening to break out of all the system's homeostatic regularity and constraint

Mr Black soon deviating within each system

System's steady state threatened by increasing morphostatic/morphogenic struggle.

System's homeostatic boundary strengthened. By Mr Black's behaviour. It becomes much more resistant to change.

Figure 6.4 *Morphostatic-morphogenic conflict*

This use of systems theory is not meant to provide understanding of all the complexities of relationships and behaviour of crisis participants. It is merely aiming to give workers an immediate mental grasp of wider conflicting processes both before and during the crisis eruption. This enables the worker to elicit some form and meaning from a situation often characterised by chaos, panic, and an unholy clamour for removal, which at the outset, can be quite overwhelming. Rather than 'reconciling very opposite', and 'soothing every passion', the concepts and jargon of systems theory can be used to do the contrary: accentuate the inherently conflictual nature of crises.

It is now time for the social worker to enter this particular crisis situation, and time .to focus upon the clients' perceptions of the same.

Clients' perceptions in crisis situations

Perceptual intervention

It is quite clear that very high hopes and expectations are being vested in the social worker even before the referral is made. Mrs Jay has not suddenly woken up one morning and decided that she was going to contact the department. As the diagram illustrates, the crisis point has been reached over many days, discussions, tensions, and previous crises, in which social services has increasingly played a role in shaping the perceptions of some of the crisis participants. Let us imagine that the social worker responds to this referral by telling Mrs Jay that he will visit immediately, without (a) making further enquiries, (b) clarifying precisely the department's responsibilities and limitations in matters of this kind, and the most important of all (c) emphasising his own neutrality in the dispute. It will then be assumed by Mrs Jay, that the social worker accepts her version of events, visiting specifically to see if he can help in the way Mrs Jay has envisaged. Mrs Jay will be relieved and her hopes will be raised. This will have a positive effect upon her own family, and upon Mr and Mrs Hammond. But it could have an adverse effect upon the greater crisis situation. Mrs Jay is certain to let Mrs Hammond know of this response by the social worker. They may then feel vindicated in getting Mr Black removed from their homes — whether the manner and means were insensitive or not; and, more importantly, their alliance could be strengthened, their hostility towards Mr Black increased, and their determination to have him removed from the home of Mrs Smith intensified, irrespective of whether Mrs Smith does or does not feel as strongly about the matter as they do. The obvious danger here is that if Mrs Jay feels more confident and determined on hearing the social worker is coming to her home, she may be encouraged to 'have another go' at Mr Black; during which she may reveal that the social worker is coming at her request, convincing him that the worker is on her side; and ensuring an ugly confrontation when he arrives.

In systems terms, such a chain of events would mean that

the social worker subsystem (before the worker has even left the office) has been absorbed by the very hostile morphostatic neighbourhood system, the principle goal of which is to rid itself of an increasingly alienated morphogenic subsystem. (Remember that the morphostatic/morphogenic struggle should not be interpreted as the parental/child generation gap. All social workers will know that in 'plea-for-removal of the elderly' crises, the elderly person's behaviour can be frighteningly morphogenic!). The worker has implicitly and unintentionally expressed his support of this principal goal and would rightly be shocked to learn that his initial response has caused what might be termed a 'perceptual intervention' of the worst possible kind, This is illustrated in Figure 6.5.

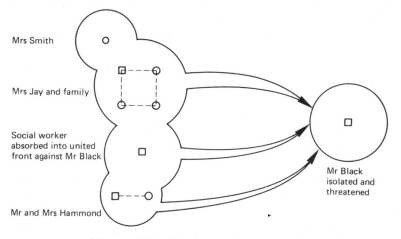

Figure 6.5   *Perceptual intervention*

Such an intervention, be it only perceptual rather than real, may dangerously increase the deviation of the morphogenic subsystem, Mr Black. He faces destitution once again, and if he perceives the powerful 'man from the welfare' firmly ensconced in the enemy camp, he may feel he has nothing more to lose. Furthermore, since his mental state is already being questioned by Mrs Jay, there is the more frightening prospect of GP, psychiatrist, and police joining the same camp.

Thus an initially poor response by the social worker has made the crisis far worse. He has exacerbated the tensions, increased suspicions and hostilities, and magnified the imbalance of power between the various subsystems. He has grossly distorted clients' perceptions about the nature of the crisis and the ways in which it might be resolved. He has overall achieved the very opposite of the fundamental goal of systems-orientated crisis intervention, which is to re-establish a supportive family and social context for the individual at the centre of the crisis. And, as we already know, he has not even visited yet!

Self-knowledge in crisis situations

Social work principles and crisis realities

Throughout this text, implicitly and explicitly, I have attempted to make the point that the level of self-awareness in crisis situations is a crucial determinant of the quality of crisis intervention service which is being offered. The following section therefore, will explore this factor in more detail. It will be done with the aid of a hypothesis about developments in this same case of Mr Black. In the process, we will get a very clear picture of the challenge which self-awareness poses; but in the end we will construct a conceptual framework which will enable the worker to surmount the challenge, and which will take its rightful prominent place in the new theoretical foundations for crisis training.

An unexpected development

Sure enough, Mrs Jay has not only informed Mrs Hammond that the social worker is coming, but she has also invited the good lady and her husband to her home in time for his arrival. She has also 'rescued' her mother from that 'dangerous man next door'. Her son Gary (17) is there too. When the social worker arrives, he immediately senses the solidarity of this group; their antagonism towards Mr Black, and their conviction that the social worker is on their side. They expect results from him. This pressure compels him to make another blunder. He invites Mrs Jay, who is obviously the group 'leader' and spokesperson, to 'go over some of the points she made in the telephone referral'. Mrs Jay unleashes a barrage of insults directed against Mr Black, and invites Mr and Mrs Hammond and her son to support her at certain strategic points. The social worker cannot get a word in. He is appalled at all this anger directed against an old man, but on the other hand he thinks; has not this tiny neighbourhood bent over backwards to accommodate this destitute man and has the latter not abused their generosity. The social worker's ability to think contrasts sharply with his inability to do anything whilst these mounting waves of passionate anger submerge him. In this atmosphere, he knows there is not a hope in hell's chance of interviewing Mrs Smith, who sits there, silently, like everybody else, compelled to listen to her daughter. Ironically, Mrs Smith is supposed to be the central victim in this crisis. He also anticipates with trepidation the reaction of Mrs Jay should he dare to suggest interviewing her mother and Mr Black together, in Mrs Smith's next-door home. He does not suggest this, but waits until he thinks the anger has subsided. Then he tries to interview Mrs Smith, but her daughter towers over her, answers virtually every question on her behalf, seeks agreement from Mr and Mrs Hammond who enthusiastically respond, and poor Mrs Smith nods helplessly.

The social worker cannot bear this much longer. He knows he should interview Mrs Smith and Mr Black in Mrs Smith's own home. But he has neither the confidence nor the means to influence the existing situation in which he finds himself, a powerful and vigourous cohesive group dominated by Mrs Jay. The social worker wants to escape now. It is not just from the awful Mrs Jay, but more to escape from his own sense of helplessness and his failure to provide Mrs Smith with the opportunity of speaking her own mind in her own way in her own home. The social worker eventually plucks up the courage to say that he will now see Mr Black. But it is something of a false courage, because he knows that he is really only using Mr Black to escape from Mrs Jay and his own sense of helplesness, and he realises that Mr Black, surely aware now of how much he has been got at by this crowd, will regard him with the utmost suspicion. The social worker, now laden with guilt as well as a sense of helplessness, goes from one home to the next and knocks the door. There is no reply. He knocks again. No reply. He is convinced Mr Black is in, because Mrs Smith said she had just left him there. He shouts in through the letter box. No response. He feels stupid. He knows that every move he makes is being observed by the group next door. He does not know what to do. He knows what he would like to do: walk away.

The unpleasantness of crisis situations

This social worker is not a buffoon. Nor is he an inherently immoral person. There is not a practising social worker in this country who will not empathise to some extent with him, because every social worker will recall their own integrity and their profession's principles being challenged in similar unpleasant crisis situations. For example, when clients yell and insult you; when they accuse you of wanting to put someone away; when they grab you with both hands and plead to be understood; when the children of clients scream in fear; when someone departs in a rage and nearly takes the door with them; or, when you are physically prevented from leaving such a Goddam awful mess.

Crisis situations are often entirely unpredictable, and pose all kinds of novel and unpleasant challenges which can provoke equally unanticipated and unprincipled responses in the social worker. If the social worker on Mrs Smith's doorstep eventually responds to Mr Blacks' justifiable paranoia, by ordering the police to force an entry, and, if, as would be quite possible, Mr Black physically resists, then what more proof does one need that the man is dangerously mad and needs to be locked up!

What then can be done about these periodical threats to

upholding a personal integrity and professional principles in crisis work? Social workers have a responsibility themselves to seek out their own potential fear, prejudice, panic, cowardice, stupidity, immorality and consequential incompetence in crisis situations. Discovering, recognising, and acknowledging these dangerous vulnerabilities are the first and major step in minimising and controlling them. Social workers need a guide for this hazardous journey. That guide should consist in the main of all past unpleasant and unsuccessful crisis experiences. From that, the worker can construct a framework enabling them to focus on the precise reasons for that unpleasantness and failure. The following frameworks, based upon my own explorations over a decade, may not be relevant to some; but if they encourage workers to construct their own, they will have served a useful purpose.

Professional and moral vulnerability in crisis intervention

A conceptional framework for exploration

The following frameworks are constructed on the broadly based perspectives of: environmental context, type of crisis, and time factor. The place in which the crisis occurs, the type of crisis it is, and the time at which the worker is asked to intervene, are all factors which can challenge the worker's professional standards and personal integrity in various ways.

These frameworks are neither comprehensive nor complete. There are many more types of crises in certain settings at certain times, in which workers have experienced their own unique vulnerabilities. And the empty last column is of course the most crucial one, in which no one should be arrogant enough to construct or answer questions on behalf of anyone else. The frameworks and their questions will provoke varying responses. Social workers who believe they are wholly competant in crisis intervention may find them insulting; students, inexperienced workers, and others, may find them too challenging. It is hoped that the majority will accept them as a helpful aid for crisis preparedness.

Table 6.1 The social/environmental context of crisis

The Setting	The Conditions: physical, social and individual(s) The source of pressure/of discomfort	Self-Exploration: exploring the impact	Does the impact make it difficult for me to uphold integrity and principle? If so, how might that vulnerability manifest itself against the client?
Urban Slum	Overcrowded, smelly. Blatant hostility and aggression. Inarticulate uneducated clients yelling at each other and prepared to listen to no one.	Is this the kind of scene likely to overwhelm me? What factors adversely affect me most: noise? aggression? the stench? the number of crisis participants? Do the appalling hygiene conditions prevent me from physically consoling client?	?
Residential Home	Residential staff's ambiguous feelings to seek help from outsider (i.e. the standby duty social worker) angry and humiliated at having to seek such help.	Which is likely to pre-occupy me more: the crisis revolving around the resident, or the feelings of the staff.	?
Hospital Casualty Department	An environment offering warmth, food and comfort; above all, the efficiency of doctors and nurses dealing with the physical injuries inflicted during the crisis. They expect social workers to be equally effective in solving the emotional and social aspect of the crisis.	What way should I respond to these expectations? Am I likely to try to convey the impression that I too will be as effective as the doctors and nurses, even though I do not feel that way at all.	?

The Setting	The Conditions: physical, social and individual(s) The source of pressure/ of discomfort	Self-Exploration: exploring the impact	Does the impact make it difficult for me to uphold integrity and principle? If so, how might that vulnerability manifest itself against the client?
Psychiatric Hospitals	Psychiatrists, with all the confidence one feels in their own clinical setting. The psychiatrist disagrees with your assessment.	Can I remain confident in my own assessment? Will I adhere to whatever decision/opinion I originally expressed?	?
Police Station	Police anxious to have client(s) removed. They have done their mercy/social bit.	Do I believe that a police station is the most inappropriate place for a client(s) in crisis? Am I likely to be influenced by the pressure and anxiety of the police?	?

Table 6.2 The crisis event

The Client	The Crisis	Likely Crisis Participants	Self-Exploration: exploring the impact	Does the impact make it difficult for me to uphold integrity and principle? If so, how might that vulnerability manifest itself against the client?
Adolescent	Parent/step-parents want the client removed after physical conflict.	Family School staff Police	Am I inhibited by the physical height/weight and/or brutality of the step-father? Am I scared or too anxious?	?
Elderly confused	Wandering, creating fire risk. Unclear. Unfed.	Relatives, Neighbours, GP, Police, Housing Department.	The sheer weight of numbers in this kind of crisis can be considerable; lay persons and professionals; will I be overwhelmed by their anxieties and pressures which they apply?	?
Married Couple	Violence. Wife battering. Wife terrified of her husband finding out she has been to social services.	Relatives, GP, Housing Department.	Am I sickened/angered/ frightened by the injuries inflicted? Will I recommend a drastic course of action without interviewing the husband?	?

Table 6.3 The time factor

Time/Day/Significant Dates or Periods	The Crisis	Conditions, for both social worker and client	Self-Exploration: exploring the impact	Does the impact make it difficult for me to uphold integrity and principle? If so, how might that vulnerability manifest itself against the client?
12.15 midday. Fifteen minutes before lunch.	A family made homeless by fire.	*Clients*: panic-stricken. *Social worker* – a very tiring morning and a very empty stomach.	Am I too tired and hungry to be able to provide the emotional support and whole hearted commitment which this family needs immediately? Am I overwhelmed by the sheer scale of the crisis?	?
4.45 pm any day	The home placement of an adolescent girl has erupted in violence.	*Clients*: angry frightened; demanding immediate help. *Social worker* anticipating a 'long job' and not wanting to miss out on that meal, night out, sports event, etc.	Will I be able to pacify them? Can I resolve the crisis without having to return the client? Can I work objectively or effectively if my mind continually wanders towards the 'goodies' that I am missing?	?

The Client	The Crisis	Likely Crisis Participants	Self-Exploration: exploring the impact	Does the impact make it difficult for me to uphold integrity and principle? If so, how might that vulnerability manifest itself against the client?
Mentally Ill	Bizzare, disturbing behaviour	Family, GP, Psychiatrist, Neighbours.	What is my general attitude and approach to the mentally ill? Do they discomfort/ frighten me? If so, how then do I react to the pressures and pain of family/relatives and professionals involved?	?
Mentally handicapped Physically handicapped	Parental/mother breakdown in caring.	Family, GP.	What is my general attitude/ approach to the mentally/physically handicapped? Can I/do I try to communicate with them? Do I think it is important enough to try to communicate with them? If I have to accommodate them elsewhere do I consider distance to be important?	?

Time/Day/Significant Dates or Periods	The Crisis	Conditions, for both social worker and client	Self-Exploration: exploring the impact	Does the impact make it difficult for me to uphold integrity and principle? If so, how might that vulnerability manifest itself against the client?
3am Standby Duty	Request for compulsory admission to psychiatric hospital of client medically assessed as mentally ill.	*Client:* hallucinating. Violent impulses. *Family:* distressed and frightened. *Social worker:* exhausted, disorientated, stranger to the area in which client lives.	Does this early hour and my unfamiliarity with the area and my inexperience in mental health matters all make it difficult (or impossible) for me to make an objective assessment? How does it affect my relationship with family members and other professionals involved.	?
Near the end of my shift in the emergency duty team. I am off for the next four days.	Any crisis in which I have invested a good deal of time and emotional/physical and mental energy.	*Client:* greatly appreciates what I have done; they have related well to me, and trust me to return tomorrow. *Social worker:* relieved to be finishing shift. Has no intentions of returning tomorrow though it is obviously the right thing to do.	How do I cope with this dilemma? I know that follow up within 24 hours by the same worker is a crucially important principle in crisis intervention, but I will not do it. Will I try to undermine the client's confidence in me by saying my colleagues will be just as good?	?

Conclusion

In this chapter I have attempted to provide a foundation upon which the bricks and mortar of an effective crisis intervention provision by individual social workers can be securely laid. The foundation consists of the discipline of family therapy, a theory of crisis derived from systems theory; an understanding and acute awareness of the power of clients' perceptions in crisis situations, and a conceptual framework for enabling social workers to explore their own vulnerabilities in crisis work. Crisis intervention in social services usually necessitates family crisis intervention. But the families in crisis served by social workers are more often than not dismembered, one-parent, reconstituted, poverty-stricken, and inarticulate, unlikely to respond to any intervention, unless it is immediate, brief, and promises to be effective. When a worker intervenes, that intervention becomes a crucial component part of the crisis system: which is why his or her condition, in terms of knowledge, experience, competence, self-awareness, and integrity, is a vitally important factor in determining the crisis outcome. One aspect of the integrity of a worker is personal, the other professional. Both refer to the values and principles which the worker and his profession regard as paramount. The complexities of crisis situations and the pressures generated by the usually high number of anxiety – laden participants can threaten the social worker's integrity. But a rigourous self-exploration of one's vulnerabilities in crisis situations is a necessary and effective first step towards the goal of upholding that integrity.

7

'I Don't Want To Lose My Baby'

Introduction

It is now time for action; time to leave our desks and immerse ourselves, confidently, determinedly, in the chaotic crises of clients in their homes, on their streets,amongst their families, friends and neighbours. In the following case history, I will continue focusing upon significant characteristics of the family and environmental contexts: the poverty, vitality, chaos, fear, anger and distress; and upon the demands and pressures made by numerous crisis participants, including other agencies. It will be seen how characteristics like these dictate to some extent the course of the crisis, and how the social worker may and does respond. The impact of clients' perceptions of the social worker will be described – so often a destructive impact. The order of theory will be imposed upon the chaos, revealing patterns in relationships, processes and communication. And family therapy principles and techniques will be used to enhance the quality of both. Finally, the narrative will highlight those moments of greatest moral and professional vulnerability during the intervention process.

Two points have to be made. First, what follows is a descriptive account of crisis intervention, interspersed with analytical commentary. It is no part of the aim of this book to deal with the gaping social and political deprivations in which the crisis erupts. Secondly, there is substantial dialogue in this intervention. The lack of video is a major disadvantage when attempting to convey the most accurate account to the reader. I can only say that my interest in crisis work over a decade has imposed certain disciplines. One of my crucially important tools for crisis study, is a pocket recorder, in which I always attempt to record seconds after leaving the crisis scene. There is no guarantee that every word of the substantial dialogue which follows actually was spoken. But I can guarantee that it is not a distorted account of the intervention process and the resolution is given in the knowledge that having made contact with the client in question long after the crisis, that same resolution has held.

The crisis referral

An urgent telephone call from the health visitor stated that Sheila, aged 20, an unmarried mother, had been thrown out of the home of Mr and Mrs Moore, who were caring for Sheila's two month old baby Carl. Previously to that, Sheila had been thrown out of her parent's home, not so much for being pregnant, as for giving birth to a 'coloured' child. Nothing was known of the father except that he was an Asian who had stopped overnight at the local Selby dockland, and had not been seen since. Sheila had an older sister, unmarried, with two children, fortunate enough to have been given a tenancy in another part of the county. Sheila had wanted to move in with her, but the housing department, having had numerous problems over the years with the whole family, were unsympathetic, and neither sister wanted to jeopardise the tenancy. The Moores willingly took Sheila in, but now they were alleging that Sheila had neglected her baby, failing to wash, feed and clothe it properly. They had now assumed 'parental responsibility' and that was that!

On leaving the Moores' home, Sheila had apparently wandered about desperately for a while. She was now temporarily being cared for by a neighbour of the Moores', Mrs Walters. The health visitor said that she had seen the baby and that the Moores were caring for it adequately. She had discussed it with the GP. They were apprehensive about what might happen next; it seemed as though a lot of the neighbours were involved, and Sheila was quite desperate at the moment, creating all kinds of problems for Mrs Walters. The health visitor and GP wanted social services to 'be involved'. They thought it might be a good idea to remove the baby for a while, until things were sorted out. Within the next hour, two similar referrals were made, one from Mrs Walters herself, and one from the probation service. Sheila had once been on a community service order for a number of minor offences. The probation officer wanted social services to know of 'the problem' concerning the child. Mrs Walters merely pleaded for help.

Initial reaction and first contact

It is helpful when one gets a referral like this, to spend a few moments in a quiet room (sitting in the car will do). The referrers collectively were displaying an anxiety which could not have been all that greater than that of those at the centre of the crisis; a little solitude, pondering the impact of the referral, helps one to counter the transference of anxiety; it may even afford a little amusement.

I chose to visit the baby's mother, Sheila, first. But when I arrived at the home of Mrs Walters, she had fled. Mrs Walters told me Sheila could not face me, and she was also frightened to go near the Moores and all their friends. Everybody had been telling her 'the social worker would take the baby off her'. The health visitor had 'warned' her a number of times. I asked Mrs Walters to find Sheila and to reassure her that I had no intentions of listening to this 'everybody'; I did have to see mother and baby, and if mother refused to return, it really was not the best way of ensuring that she kept her baby. In the meantime I would visit the Moores, who were expecting me.

Mr and Mrs Moore, in their grotty, smelly home, with bare floors, unopened rotting windows, and very little furniture, nevertheless appeared to provide some kind of informal 'community centre' for the benefit of unemployed, single parents and school absconders in the neighbourhood. But it was not the ideal kind of community centre: through the haze of thick smoke I counted no less than twelve persons, most of them on the floor, virtually rubbing shoulders with each other. I imagined them sitting there most of the day; just sitting, smoking, drinking tea, coming in and out as they pleased. The group was dominated by Mrs Moore. She sat by the fireside, with baby Carl lying contentedly in her arms. Three adolescent girls sat around her knees, each of them on occasion trying to engage the baby's attention. Her husband sat opposite. Everyone stared at me silently and suspiciously when I entered.

'Good Lord!' I said. 'I didn't realise you had such a big family Mrs Moore'. I remained standing, smiling, and looked around at every member of the group, making it obvious by manner and tone that I really did not believe they were all members of the same family. Some thought I did believe that; but others detected the mild irony; in either case it provoked reciprocal smiles, and Mrs Moore's compulsion to explain.

'They're just friends. . .they live around here.'

'Oh. . .I see, how about introducing me?'

This she did. Their ages ranged approximately from fourteen to thirty. The Moores were not much older. I looked and spoke to each one as I was introduced, still conveying the impression that I regarded this enormous group as something of an amusing novelty. The initial tension which greeted my entry reduced rapidly. It seemed as though they had expected some officious authority type figure to make a pronouncement to the Moores about the infant.

'Now this is really difficult Mrs Moore. . . .' I said, finding myself a space to sit.

She looked at me, puzzled.

'I'm sure all these friends of yours know what's going on. . .but there's so many of them. I'm not sure if it's right for me to begin talking about this problem whilst all of you folk remain here. And yet I can't ask them to leave. . .they've more of a right to be here than me. They're your friends'.

I repeatedly looked around the group as I spoke. I could see that my words were having varying impacts on each of them. I maintained a silent, questing, and curious stance which was certain to increase the pressure upon them for some kind of response. Eventually two older members of the group responded almost simultaneously: 'Let's go', they said, slowly and reluctantly getting up from the floor. I spoke a few words to nearly all of them as they made their way to the back door. I expressed my gratitude a number of times, and, when they had gone, I turned to Mrs Moore and apologised for all the disruption I was causing.

Analysis and comment (1)

The most striking characteristic of this crisis, typical of many, is its conflictual nature. It is easy to imagine the preceding events: confrontations, violence, walkouts (or even throwouts). These events, in which powerful perceptions of social services obviously played a part, have generated an enormous degree of hostile expectancy for the social worker's visit. But the worker does not fulfil those expectations. Much to their surprise, the worker does not look, speak, act, or think like the stern authority figure they had braced themselves for. Even more puzzling, he apparently treats them with some deference, and at the same time reaches out to each of them in a spontaneous, warm and humourous manner. Ironically, this technique affords him a far more effective 'authority' than the one they had envisaged, and were prepared to resist.

There is however, a risk involved. Mrs Moore desperately wants that group to stay. The worker's success in getting them to leave creates a certain tension between Mrs Moore and himself. But throughout, the worker has repeatedly recognised and respected her status in the group, made it plain that he would not attempt to usurp her authority by telling them or demanding that they leave. Note that whilst he reaches out to the group, his words are nevertheless emphasising her pivotal and most influential position in the group. Any insistence by Mrs Moore therefore that her friends remain, would seem to all grossly unreasonable.

Systems perspective (1)

This group of people constitutes one of those unhealthy 'open' crisis systems (see page 62) commonly found in the notorious pockets of run-down estates, where there is an abnormally high level of unemployment and poverty. Such a system knows few boundaries and sets even fewer. There is a massive and ceaseless input from the surrounding neighbourhood system. In normal times, this need be no cause for concern; indeed, many may depend upon it. But the events and processes leading up to the crisis, and the crisis eruption itself, have turned the overall neighbourhood system on its head. A compassionate reaching out has been replaced by a seemingly cruel banishment; care of mother and child has been replaced by victimisation of the former and a virtual theft of the latter; what was probably an easy-going fun and variety-laden group that daily assembles in the Moores', has become a hostile suspicious group entrenched in the view that Sheila was wholly to blame for the crisis. This then, is the condition of a new potentially explosive system totally dominated by morphostatic forces. It can 'blow' any second if the wrong person comes to the door; if a tactless word is spoken; or if a threatening action is taken. It may be represented like this:

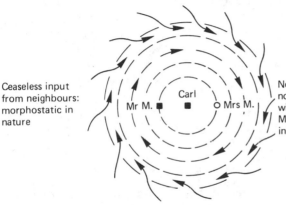

Ceaseless input from neighbours: morphostatic in nature

Carl
Mr M. ■   ■   ○ Mrs M.

No output from system nor healthy interchange with external environment. Morphostatic forces intensifying.

Figure 7.1

Note that the infant subsystem, though new and novel, offers no threat to this system; it is powerless and has been easily absorbed. The mother subsystem has not, presumably because her goals are incompatible with the system's, particularly those of Mr and Mrs Moore. At this moment in time, the system's defence mechanism (negative feedback) is most alert, because it anticipates a morphogenic threat (social worker) arising from its expulsion of the subsystem (Sheila). The new social worker subsystem has a major impact on the crisis system. It behaves in such a way that it is not only accepted by the system, but manages to acquire a position of power and influence within it. It then sets about dismantling the crisis system (the first step of which is to get rid of the neighbours), and attempt to replace that system with one that is entirely different.

No doubt the neighbours will drift back to the Moores when the social worker has left, but crisis intervention demands the speedy construction of an alternative system in which enlightenment, mutual tolerance and sensitivity, can withstand the trends and pressures towards a return to the hopelessness and destructiveness of the crisis state. Social work writers who advocate systems theory are inclined to think of systems having a fair degree of permanency about them. Their diagrams refer to a particular social or family set of circumstances which have arisen over a period of weeks or years. In crisis intervention however, the worker must be prepared to think and act in response to systems which are changing literally by the moment. More importantly, they have to be able to bring about those changes themselves. As has been demonstrated, it need not be a frightening insurmountable task. Ugly, destructive crisis systems can be dismantled by the simplest of gestures, the minimum of words, and the least possible threat.

Moral and professional vulnerability (1)

Readers will note that the worker in this instance is not the frightened, bungling, incompetent of earlier chapters, and that his success in getting Mrs Moore's entourage to leave probably depended upon (a) detailed knowledge of the community, (b) experience, and (c) family therapy techniques for deflating tension and hostility. Readers may justifiably ask therefore: can I achieve the same result if I have not got the same knowledge, experience and technique? The answer is, most certainly, but only if there has been sufficient self-awareness gained through the kind of conceptual framework offered in the previous chapter. Preparation for crisis work means being aware of how certain characteristics of the crisis situation, for instance, the large number of people, the smoke-filled room, the hostile atmosphere, and so on, can make it difficult to act in the way that you know and feel is morally and professionally right. That kind of self-awareness is potentially more valuable than any knowledge, experience and technique, because it gives rise to an integrity of purpose which will ensure that you will at least attempt to do what is right. And it can be done more simply and directly than was demonstrated. The social worker who is nervous and inexperienced, (but aware of it) should fix his eyes on Mrs Moore, move close to her, and say something to the effect: 'I need to speak to you and your husband alone'. Nothing more is needed at that initial stage, except that he should keep his eyes on Mrs Moore until she responds. If she protests or refuses (which in my experience would be unlikely) the worker must repeat himself. If other members of the group try to engage his attention or even challenge him, he should repeat himself again as an explanation: for instance, 'I'm sorry, but I came here to speak to Mr and Mrs Moore alone.' If he still does not get the required response, he should withdraw, emphasising to Mrs Moore that he will have to report her refusal to have a proper discussion about the infant, Carl.

When social workers enter a crisis situation they will encounter many obvious wrongs. The unpleasant crisis conditions may tempt them to avoid these, or even compel them to add to these wrongs by thought, word or deed. Of course it would be easier to discuss Sheila's case in the presence of twelve people you do not know how to shift. But what would be the likely outcome? Would it not be the most effective way of ensuring that Sheila never returned, and strengthening those worse possible perceptions she has of the worker in the first instance? Like most easy and unprincipled actions it merely compounds the crisis by exacerbating its suspicions and hostilities, and guarantees a resolution far less satisfactory than that you are trying to achieve.

Replacing the crisis system: space, balance and order

Mrs Moore barely moved as the room emptied. The baby never stirred during the commotion, sleeping soundly in her firm, gentle embrace. I made a few jokey remarks about her hospitality, trying to put her at ease a little now that she was bereft of such a formidable support, and before attempting the next task of getting Sheila to join us. When I put this suggestion to both of them, they said they did not mind having Sheila there. But Mrs Moore's hold of the baby tightened.

Mrs Walters had, as expected, found Sheila. It was not difficult to persuade her to return now that the group she regarded as so hostile had left. We walked to the Moores' together. She appeared quite lost. I did not think she was aware, like me, of the neighbours peering at us through their windows. When we got to the Moores', she ignored my request to sit near Mrs Moore and myself. She sat in the furthest corner of the room and held her head low so that her long, black hair completely covered her face. Her fingers clenched tightly and she fidgeted a lot. She never looked at her child.

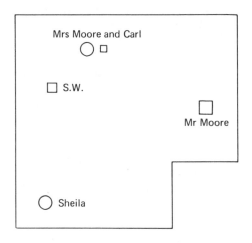

Figure 7.2

The diagram gives some indication of the tension which Sheila's entrance created. This seating arrangement was quite useless for proceeding with any meaningful discussions. It had to be altered. But there was a far more difficult and immediate task to perform: to get Mrs Moore to hand over the infant to its mother. Sheila had returned to the home with great apprehension. I had to avoid prolonging the humiliation she must have been enduring in being separated from her child. But in order to carry out this task, I had to sit as closely as possible to Mrs Moore and give the impression that I was ignoring Sheila. As Mrs Moore testified on all of Sheila's misdemeanours, I knew that Sheila herself was seething.

S. W.: It's very commendable, Mrs Moore, you taking on that kind of responsibility.

Mrs Moore: I've always done it...I don't mind

S. W: I can see that. You handle the baby very well.

She does not reply, but gratification is obvious as she looks down on the sleeping infant.

S. W: And all these people...Are they here often? Do they just come and go as they please?

Mrs Moore: More or less, it's a free house.

S. W: Don't you ever tell them to clear off?

She shakes her head.

S. W.: (Turning to Mr Moore) What about you, Mr Moore, don't you mind all this coming and going?

Mr Moore: Not a bit. The crack's good. (He turns to his wife; they both laugh.)

S. W.: Yes, I bet it is. (After a long pause) Well I don't think this is very good. (Their smiles disappear.)

Mrs Moore: What?

S. W: What you've been talking about; you taking on all this responsibility; just like you're doing now, and there's Sheila sitting there in the corner twiddling her thumbs. (I turn round and look at Sheila, raising my voice to a louder, authoritive tone.) SHEILA, I want you to give Mrs Moore a break. You take Carl for a while.

Mrs Moore: It's all right; it's no bother...I'm...

S. W.: NO! I insist. I've heard enough. I've seen it all. Come on, Sheila, give Mrs Moore a break. Here's your child.

I stand up and move towards Sheila. I put one arm around

her and gently pressure her up and towards Mrs Moore. When she is nearly there, I let her go and step back. Mrs Moore is speechless as she hands the child over. Both women are nervous and try to handle Carl with meticulous care. Sheila is about to return to her seat.

S.W.:   How about bringing your chair nearer, Sheila. And you too Mr Moore. We seem to be very far away from each other here.

I beckoned Sheila to sit on an armchair at the other side of the fireplace, and for Mr Moore to move his chair much nearer to his wife and I. I remained very close to Mrs Moore.

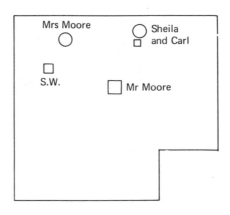

Figure 7.3

Analysis and comment (2)

It is difficult to overestimate the significance of the changes which have taken place during this phase of the intervention. When the worker arrived, Mrs Moore was in the most powerful and influential position. Sheila was in the worst possible position. Mrs Moore has been stripped of her power, first by the departure of a large body of friends who obviously hold her in high esteem, and secondly, by the removal of Carl. This psychological rape has paradoxically been made possible by the authoritative figure of the social worker continually bombarding her with compliments about her kindly, motherly disposition, and the implied suggestion that some may take advantage of it. The social worker deliberately sits near her, in order to reinforce these compliments by facial and bodily gestures, occasionally putting his hand on her shoulder, and always addressing her with warmth and respect. This is not just to cushion the blow of losing the child, but also, to convey the strongest possible impression that when the child is handed over, she can depend upon the social worker to protect her from any further exposure. The family therapy principle behind this technique has been defined by Minuchin (1974) as follows: 'any therapeutic input that challenges a dysfunctional process...must at the same time support its participants' (p.58).

Social workers probably more than anybody else, are aware of how much the physical presence of an infant can be exploited by clients, for example to impress, to divert one's attention, to prove one's point, to hide behind, to block, to ignore whatever else is happening around the infant. Then there is the less subtle, open conflict, actual tug-o-war, with all the accompanying distress of the child in the middle, and the occasional injury to the parent on either side. Generally speaking, there is no greater immorality and damage perpetrated against children, and social workers have a primary responsibility to learn how to handle such situations in the least risk-laden way possible.

Space is a potent medium for the expression of existing tensions and relationships. The social worker's success in improving the latter may be seriously hindered if he ignores the former. The difficulty for many social workers may be merely one of interpretation: that any request or move to alter existing seating arrangements is a gross infringement upon client's privacy. A more sensible interpretation would be that the pain and distress of clients in crisis is sustained and even intensified by seating arrangements. (O'Hagan, 1984). If so, an attempt should be made to alter them.

Systems perspective (2)

This intervention phase dramatically demonstrates the nature of the crisis intervention task. The social worker has in effect abolished the potentially explosive system which he entered, and has replaced it with an entirely new system, in which he is and will remain the dominant influence for the duration of the intervention task. The status and functions of the remaining subsystems have changed drastically. Their former power and weakness, support, and isolation, possession and loss have been removed or reversed and are no longer the crucial features they were in the original crisis system. The subsystem of Mrs Moore has been most seriously weakened and exposed, but the most powerful subsystem, the social worker, has chosen a position where he can ideally help her to recover,and protect her from further exposure. The weakest and most vulnerable (therefore dangerous) subsystem, Sheila, has been strengthened considerably. The possession of the infant fulfils that subsystem's most fundamental needs. And in the hands of its mother, the infant subsystem is much less the focal point of noisy, uncontrollable bickering and hostility. A subsystem (Mr Moore) which has appeared to be virtually on the periphery of the system, contributing little or nothing to the hectic transformation taking place within, has, as a first step, been asked (but in reality, compelled) to move into a position whereby it can accept more responsibility, particularly that of supporting its partner subsystem (Mrs Moore).

It would be wrong to assume that this transformation of itself, is healthy. It is, provided the social worker is going to remain there for a while and strengthen it. But like all newborns, this new system is extremely fragile in these first few moments of life. Particularly so when it is such an artificial creation, unrecognisable from the chaos, aggression and blow-ups which have obviously preceded it. It is these which have to be explored, and this new system's greatest merit is that its 'steady state' will enable the social worker to do so. From the creating of this new social system, the social worker hopes to be transported back into the old to learn of the origins of this crisis. As for the future, that may require something entirely different from either.

Professional and moral vulnerability (2)

What are the likely consequences if one does not attempt to get the infant returned to the arms of its mother? Let us explore that with the help of an alternative scenario.

The social worker, uncomfortably conscious of Sheila's isolation and separation from her infant but unable to do anything about it, invites Mrs Moore to explain why she has taken this rather extreme action. Mrs Moore replies by giving more details of Sheila's neglect, emphasising the 'salient' points by holding Carl more tightly and closely to her. Sheila listens and her anger and humiliation increase. She interrupts Mrs Moore with ugly violent yells, trying to defend herself. Mrs Moore responds: 'See, that's what I've got to put up with... look...see what's she's done!' (Carl, awakened by his mother's screams, begins to cry in Mrs Moore's arms). Sheila, now doubly humiliated by the fact that the social worker has seen her cause her infants distress, loses all control, and hurls more and more abuse at Mrs Moore, and the social worker too, whom she can now only perceive to be entirely on the side of Mrs Moore. The social worker, who began in the knowledge of and sympathy towards Sheila's plight, now thinks that perhaps Mrs Moore has a point. As Sheila's attacks on him increase, he becomes less preoccupied and less guilty about his own initial sense of helplessness. Her attacks unnerve him and provoke Mr Moore into the fray. Mr Moore makes the same allegations as his wife and defends the social worker's right to be there. Sheila can take no more. She launches at Mr Moore, verbally and physically abusing him. The social worker, tense and frightened, decides the child will have to be removed from this awful and dangerous mess. Worse still, and by no means beyond the bounds of possibility, he may decide that Mrs Moore is doing a fine job and perhaps Sheila is in need of treatment. (See O'Hagan, 1980a, for a similar tug o'war situation, in which the initial referral sought hospitalisation for a seventeen-year-old mother, derived of the physical contact of her infant in the crisis situation.)

Readers may ponder this not improbable scenario and ask; How is it to be avoided? How can one get the child returned to its mother if one does not have the confidence and technique to do so? Indeed, the description of how it was done may make some social workers more apprehensive about the nature of the task. But it should be clear now that there are equally important attributes besides confidence and technique. There is a gut reaction and professional knowledge that will tell the social worker the existing situation is very wrong. There is a personal integrity and professional principles pressurising him to do what is right. Most importantly, the social worker should now be aware of what it is in the existing situation which makes it difficult to uphold that integrity and professional principle. For example, it may be that you think Mrs Moore has given enough away in the departure of her formidable entourage, and you just have not the confidence to ask for any more; or you may have become resigned (and relieved) that Mr Moore is so passive, and you are extremely reluctant to provoke him into a defence of his wife's right to have the child. Another possibility is that the existing seating arrangements, in which your head has had to turn a full 180 degrees merely to see the participants, is not conducive to the sense of control you feel you may need before dispossessing Mrs Moore any further. There are numerous other reasons or conditions that will caution a social worker about tackling this problem. There can be no excuse for a worker not at least recognising what they are. And yet, despite their number and their nature there is an overriding consideration which conscience, personal integrity and professional principles will not let the worker forget; that in this crisis situation, a young unmarried mother, disowned by her parents, deprived of her child, sits humiliated in the cold bare corner of a squalor-ridden room, like a prisoner in the dock; and that if she remains there, there is not a hope in Hell's chance of making any progress.

All this awareness can only strengthen the worker's determination to change the situation. Confidence and technique are not essential; a determination based upon integrity and principle will do fine. Say to Mrs Moore; 'Mrs Moore give the baby to Sheila, please'; or, 'Mrs Moore, I realise you've been very helpful to this child, now I want you to give him to his mother, and I want you, Sheila, to sit over here.' It does not matter if your heart is pounding, your legs are weak, your voice is trembling, and you are afraid of making a fool of yourself. Do it because you know it is right; because you personally and the profession you represent will not tolerate the iniquity of the situation.

Strengthening the new system: a shift in focus

As soon as the seating has been rearranged, I say to the group: 'Thanks, now we can see each other without getting a creak in the neck'. I turn to Mr Moore, nod my head in the direction of his wife, and say half jokingly: 'Can't you stop this woman taking on all this work?'

Mr Moore: (emphatically): Never...she'd do a body any turn.
S.W.: What do you feel about that?
Mr Moore: Me? I just let her get on with it.
S.W.: But what do you feel about it?
Mr Moore: It's all right with me.
S.W.: But what do you feel about it?
Mr Moore: I think...
S.W.: No no! not 'think', I want to know how you 'feel' about all this kindness in your wife?
Mr Moore: (thinking for a while): 'Well...I suppose I feel good...
S.W.: But...?
Mr Moore: She gets hurt sometimes.
S.W.: Oh? How...When?
Mr Moore: Well...the last child we looked after...when its mother took it back, it died a couple of months later.

Analysis and comment (3)

The social worker begins by strengthening the new system he has created: here we all are together; we can see each other, talk to each other, and we should respect each other, whatever our differing viewpoints. Still acutely conscious of Mrs Moore's vulnerability, he vigorously pursues her husband's support and admiration of her. It is an effective diversionary tactic that takes everybody's mind – but her mind in particular – off her own sense of exposure. But (and this is so typical in crises) the social worker gets far more than he bargained for: he finds out that Mr and Mrs Moore, in all their poverty and squalour, their limited intellects and understanding, have actually been providing some kind of ghastly informal fostering for anyone unfortunate enough to need their services. Their care of infants might be impeccable – notwithstanding the comings and goings in that squalid smoke-filled room, but they have clearly demonstrated to the worker their total unsuitability for dealing with the numerous complexities of fostering, particularly those pertaining to the rights and feelings of natural parents. This becomes more obvious throughout the interview.

The 'heart' of the matter

S. W.:   You must have been shattered by that
                experience, Mrs Moore.

Mrs Moore: Yes, I was. It was thriving here, wasn't it,
                John?

Mr Moore: That's right. (Nodding in the direction of his
                wife). She cried for a week after it. She still
                cries now and again.

S. W.:   Is that why Carl means so much to you?

(It is a measure of the sense of security which the worker has restored in Mrs Moore, that he can risk focusing once again on Carl.)

Mrs Moore: I can't stand kids not being looked after.

S. W.:   No. I'm sure you can't. (Turns to Sheila.) Has
                Mrs Moore been doing most of the looking
                after, Sheila? Why?

Sheila (Clasping the baby more tightly): She does it better than me.

S. W. (With exaggerated surprise): What? (He turns to Mrs Moore.) Did you hear that?

The worker says no more for a moment. Eventually Sheila and Mrs Moore look at each other for the first time.

S. W.:   Can she do everything better than you, Sheila?
                (Sheila nods meekly.) Where does the baby
                sleep?

Sheila: With them.

S. W. :   Why?

Sheila:	Because I can never hear him.
S.W.:	Bullshit! (S.W. turns to Mrs Moore) Why's he sleeping in your room?
Mrs Moore:	Well...
Mr Moore:	Sheila never got up. We offered to bring Carl into our room.
S.W.:	Why didn't you get up Sheila?
Sheila:	I couldn't.... I just couldn't.
S.W.:	Too tired?
Sheila:	Yes.
S.W.:	Because you go to bed too late?
Sheila:	I don't know.
S.W.(Looks at Mr and Mrs Moore):	Tell me...both of you...Sheila wouldn't get up when baby needed her. That's bad. But did you really believe you were doing her a good turn by bringing baby into your room, feeding it, clothing it, nursing it all day long, letting mum do whatever she liked?
Mr Moore (Irritated):	The child had to be fed.
S.W.:	I'm not talking about the child. I'm talking about what all that kindness of yours was doing for Sheila.
Mrs Moore:	We couldn't get her to change.
S.W.:	But now she's got worse. In actual fact she's got so bad that kind people like you — and a lot of others – don't even think she's fit to have the child. Isn't that why I'm here?
Sheila (Bursting into tears):	I don't want to lose my baby...I know they're kind to me...I've never known people to be so kind to me...but I can't manage...I can't look after Carl the way Maureen (Mrs Moore) does. She even holds him better...but I don't want to lose him...I couldn't manage on my own...I'm afraid...

Analysis and comment (4)

Readers will notice that the pace has quickened considerably and the tone changed dramatically in this phase. The worker is confident he can do this because of:

(a) his firm grip on the proceedings:

(b) Sheila's sense of security in holding her child, and

(c) the most important, Mrs Moore's partial recovery from the loss of the child and all her neighbours. (The compliments continue to flow, and the social workers' objective of being replaced by Mr Moore as the principle source of her support, has been achieved).

There is therefore little need of that same degree of subtlety and delicacy in enlightening the participants, or in enhancing the relationships and communications between them. The worker feels he can do this more directly. The bluntness (which some may find offensive) is a characteristic of strategy; he has no intentions of maintaining the artificial system of timidity which he has created and dominated; it is in no one's interests if he replaces tension and hostile feelings with an unspoken yet heeded command that everyone has to be nice to everyone else. His bluntness is an unmistakable way of saying 'I want to listen to you...I want to try to help...but I'm not going to listen to a load of bull!' Of course, had he said something like this on entry, there would have been a riot.

All the preceding opinions and analyses have been reinforced during this rapid phase of the intervention. But in addition, there is the revelation that Sheila has been an unwitting victim of a cruel double bind: 'Go out, have fun, we'll look after your baby.' and 'You should be ashamed going out having fun and neglecting your baby'; and/or 'You don't need to learn how to look after your baby, we'll do it for you; You should be ashamed of yourself not being able to look after your baby.' These double binds can be made extremely effective by the subtle use of time. The first message was probably conveyed before she went out for her nights' fun; the second conflicting message when she returned. Gradually this provoked more irresponsible behaviour. The rows which followed were very one-sided affairs, Sheila invariably humiliated and defeated. Utterly confused, increasingly isolated, unable to comprehend and articulate on the cruel double bind in which she was trapped, and above all, separated from the only real meaningful possession – her own child – Sheila's eventual expulsion from the Moore home and neighbourhood was inevitable.

The therapeutic potential in crisis

In the previous chapter, caution was expressed about the principle of the therapeutic potential in crisis situations. It has been clearly demonstrated here that in these typical plea-for-removal crises, in extremely deprived communities, that potential can only be realised after a massive intervention, in which the worker has:

1. dismantled the crisis system;
2. replaced it with one in which the preceding negative and destructive communication between the crisis participants have been drastically minimised;
3. transformed the crisis atmosphere of hostility, panic and a high sense of risk, into one in which the participants feels much more secure.

When these necessary stages of the intervention are successfully completed, the worker may set about exploiting the therapeutic potential. This is largely an act of faith; a conviction that crisis participants are not wholly consumed by the hatred and fear which has characterised the crisis situation; that they are quite capable of understanding the origin of the crisis and the part they played in it, and capable of the mutual tolerance without which the crisis cannot be satisfactorily resolved. Exploiting this therapeutic potential however, should not be interpreted as working towards a resolution in which all the goals and aspirations of the crisis participants can be fulfilled. It will be obvious now that in this particular crisis, such a resolution is impossible.

Crisis resolution

Sheila held onto her child more tightly as she cried. I purposely chose not to comfort her. I wanted the Moores to do that. After a long and painful silence broken only by Sheila's tears, Mrs Moore eventually said in a trembling yet convincing voice: 'We're not going to take Carl off you, luv'; her husband repeated it. I'm sure the Moore's meant this, but

I had grave doubts about their ability to adhere to it. From the first few moments of my intervention I had this gut reaction telling me that Sheila and her child should not be here. Now as the Moores made that simple and moving declaration, I could not help feeling that the system which had evolved during the past few weeks would re-emerge again; the same desire of Mrs Moore to have Carl, the same temptation for Sheila to have a good time, the Moore's willingness to oblige, and the same ghastly over-involvement of umpteen neighbours and friends. Yet, I also felt that this was the worst possible time to share some of these thoughts. The crisis characteristics of fear and destructiveness had been replaced by mutual understanding, humility and compassion. It was a significant advance, and any depressing though realistic thoughts, no matter how tactfully conveyed, would have been grossly insensitive (possibly dangerous too: the crisis principle about living systems needing time to adapt or readapt to new situations is in operation here (See p.31). Another reason for not expressing my doubts was much more pragmatic; I had not yet had time to seek out alternative accommodation for Sheila. No matter how strongly I might have felt about her remaining there, there would not have been much point in opposing it until that alternative had been found. That was precisely how I would use the few days breathing space which this intervention had achieved. In the meantime I would help to strengthen reconciliation.

The final phase was a most pleasant one. It consisted of handing back to the crisis participants all the information they had provided so that they could construct their own task-centred plan. As has been stated before, one of the distinguishing features of crisis situations is their honesty and openness; people really do let their hair down, particularly in their own home; this is very much to be contrasted with the social services office, in which 'guarded behaviours are generated' (Everstine *et al.*, 1977). These crisis participants, Sheila and the Moores, knew exactly what had been happening. They had not been 'taught' or 'enlightened' by the social worker; on the contrary, they had enlightened him and themselves by re-enacting in the most dramatic way the actual causes of the crisis, and each scene had given the worker a deeper understanding and grasp of all the pre crisis processes.

Having re-enacted this drama, neither Sheila nor the Moores needed anyone to point out the game they had been playing with each other, nor its possible dangerous consequences. They knew that the plan they now have to devise would have to clearly specify Sheila's responsibilities for her own child, and the Moore's responsibility to encourage her, to insist on reasonable conduct regarding the number of nights she went out and the times she came in. In most interventions I extricate myself for a short while so that the crisis participants can produce this plan independently (O'Hagan, 1984). In this case however, the group needed a little support, initially taken aback as they were that the worker had no intentions of doing it for them. They completed the task, and I suggested writing the main points down in case of any memory lapse!

Within the next twenty-four hours, I had made some progress regarding possible alternative accommodation. I called again, as I said I would, and found that the drift back of all the neighbours and friends had begun. It did not appear as though it was yet undermining the reconciliation between the Moores and Sheila. On the third day, however, the Moores had some complaints to make, and a more confident assertive Sheila resented it. I mentioned possible alternatives for the first time, to which Mrs Moore, predictably, reacted by stressing 'there was no trouble at all'. Sheila, unwittingly, reinforced this by saying her parents would never have her back. I told her I was not thinking of her parents, I was thinking about her sister, and that I had already spoken to the housing department who were willing to reconsider the request that she joined her. I asked Sheila for permission to make contact with her sister. She welcomed this. Then I spoke to Mrs Moore alone. In an atmosphere entirely different from that of the crisis, I was able to persuade her to accept the inevitable. I could not alter her feelings; she was sure to miss the child greatly; but she was sensitive and realistic enough to eventually accept that Sheila and her child's interests would be better served elsewhere.

Later I visited Sheila's sister in the company of another

social worker working in that area. After hearing a detailed account of Sheila's plight since the birth of Carl, and of the recent crisis, her sister said she would be willing to have her, provided Housing approved. We reassured her they did. We were under no illusions about the task ahead. But the mature, married (mother of three children) social worker who was now taking over from me had a much better chance of success in enabling Sheila, with the help of community health services – midwifery and health visitor – to learn basic skills in infant management, and accepting the discipline and responsibility it would necessitate. Sheila and Carl moved in with her sister a week later. But not before Mrs Moore phoned the office to say she couldn't cope any more, and enquiring about the date of Sheila's departure! Two years later, Sheila and Carl are still living with her sister. There have been periodic reviews, all concluding that she is caring adequately for her son.

8

Ethical Considerations for Crisis Intervention

Introduction

The previous chapter represented a final stage, a logical culmination giving potent expression and practical demonstration of many of the lessons the author has learnt in more than a decade's experience of crisis intervention in a social services department. But in no sense can it be regarded as a conclusion; on the contrary, it has perhaps raised more contentious questions than all the preceding chapters put together. A particular kind of morality has been emphasised. It necessitates brave decisions and actions under very difficult circumstances. But there is another kind of morality at issue here, a morality well established in the social work tradition. It is concerned with the social worker's use of power, authority and control, the persuasive and manipulative features of family therapy techniques; the fundamental social work principles of respect for clients, acceptance of them and their right to self-determination. Can such principles and rights be upheld in the kind of intervention advocated? Should social workers exercise power, authority and control in crisis situations? Can manipulation of clients ever be justified? Before attempting to answer such questions, it is necessary to examine the origins of the moral theory underpinning many of those social works principles.

Powerful social worker; powerless client!

One of the most prominent features of the deluge of social work literature of the sixties and early seventies was a preoccupation with moral questions arising out of client – worker interactions. This preoccupation stemmed chiefly from an acute social work sensitivity to the imbalance of power between worker and client.

> Of all professions in contact with the poor, only social workers in their training learn to understand the significance of this factor in their relationships. They recognise the importance of guarding professionalism against functioning as a disequalising force. (Titmuss, 1965, p.364)

Social work texts emphasised that whilst the worker was generally educated, articulate, and socially sophisticated, their clients were mostly uneducated, inarticulate, and lacking in basic social skills. The moral dangers in this imbalance were explored through numerous and diverse perspectives: for instance, through a religious perspective (Biestek, 1961); philosophical (Plant, 1970); political (Jordan, 1974); and through a basically pragmatic social work itself (Timms, 1964; Younghusband, 1967). From such explorations came a reassertion of such moral principles as the clients' right to self-determination, respect for clients, acceptance of them, and the recognition of their innate dignity and worth.

But what do such principles mean in the context of the crisis situations we have been discussing? And how would such principles be applied and upheld? Those early moral and philosophical explorations quite clearly took place within the relatively tiny arena of a casework relationship, that is, a relationship between a single worker and a single client. In contrast, the crisis situations we have been discussing have all been characterised by an arena unlimited in size, and by a large number of participants in which the worker might well have difficulty in identifying a single client. Those who have criticised family therapy on moral grounds have not faced up to this reality. Their criticisms rest entirely on the sound basis of the inalienable rights of the individual, and the ethical principles of social work which uphold those rights. This morality Whan (1983) suggests, 'involves us in a critical self reflexive process of evaluation' in which both worker and client should have the opportunity to engage in a 'self consciousness process of reasoning'; a conversation that allows worker and client to 'exercise more fully their human selves; to question, reflect, speak, listen and be heard, and to agree or differ with what is said' (p.333).

There can be no doubt that this civilised communication is infinitely superior in any moral sense to family therapy's manipulative techniques and to a philosophy of crisis intervention which stresses clients' dependancy upon the worker. Most social workers indeed, would be greatly relieved if all their interactions with clients were conducive to that 'self-consciousness process of reasoning'. The initial stage of a social worker's entry into a family crisis certainly is not so conducive, and it would be astonishingly naïve and dangerous for anyone to think so. Even less appropriate is such a stage for the encouragement of individuals to 'exercise more fully their human selves'; and any social worker who begins intervention by being absolutely honest about the sources of panic, chaos and suffering being inflicted all around him, is very unlikely to reach any other stage in the intervention process.

The manipulative techniques which Whan (1983) and Wright (1981) criticise, are a means of exercising power in the crisis situation. Power, authority and control are crucially important tools for the crisis worker. But before discussing this contentious issue further, it may be instructive to underline some of these more unpleasant features of crisis which the proponents of 'armchair casework morality' have perhaps never encountered.

The ugly face of crisis

The inalienable rights of whom?

Individuals suffer in crisis situations. The vast majority of social work crises are fundamentally conflictual in nature: individual(s) against individual(s) against family, group, agency or community, and in the case of mental illness crises, the conflict between madness and sanity (Bott, 1976). Individuals intentionally inflict suffering upon each other preceding and during the crises. The systematic battering of the step-child is often a response to the step-child's deliberate attempt to humiliate the step-parent. The lone elderly person's more outrageous behaviour towards his elderly neighbours is in response to their campaign to get him removed. The mother's desertion of her husband and children is a desperate protest at her being treated like a slave. These are examples in which the disputing sides may be evenly matched; matched in the sense that each is capable of inflicting suffering on the other. But when conflicts degenerate to the crisis level at which it is decided to ask a social worker to intervene, the sides are not likely to be evenly matched. Crisis situations are unique in their honesty and openness. One immediately identifies the losing side. The final stages of the conflict are often painful to watch. The loser is isolated (or, like Mr Black and Sheila, they have already been shoved out). If the social worker was only to sit back, watch and listen, he would see nothing more than the continual intensifying humiliation of the loser, and of course, he would be asked to condone it, and, in many cases, to deliver the final blow by statutory removal. In these conflictual crises, it would be a privilege indeed if the worker had only one moral obligation, to uphold the dignity and the inalienable rights of one individual client. The reality of crisis situations however, is very different. The worker will often be faced with a bewildering array of conflicting moral dilemmas and statutory obligations regarding numerous clients. As Jordan and Packman (1978) remark: 'The turbulence generated in such families is extremely demanding and exhausting for the worker. He feels himself torn between the needs and feelings of differing members' (p.337). The experienced worker therefore, knows that whatever decision he makes, whatever action he takes, and whatever the outcome of the crisis, he will at some point have acted against the will and the 'dignity' and the inalienable rights of some crisis participant(s), and possibly against the wishes of them all. The idea of consensus democracy and equality between worker and individual client does not easily apply to the reality of family crisis situations.

Violence in crisis situations

Another feature the worker will observe on occasions is actual physical violence. The violence could well be directed against the worker. Social workers have been murdered, raped, attacked and humiliated by clients; 'eaten for breakfast' as Speed *et al.* (1982) metaphorically puts it, by what Jordan (1981) realistically calls 'brutish' clients. The crisis of the client then becomes much more of a crisis of the worker. Some crisis situations can be so dangerous that the worker's most sensible course of action is to 'run like hell' (Jordan and Packman, 1978, p.335). A colleague of long standing in Selby, fortunately a very mature and experienced social worker, once dealt with a crisis of alleged incest between a father and daughter. She confronted the father with this allegation, made by amongst others, his wife who had recently left him.During the confrontation, my colleague had an overwhelming sense of danger about this man. She refused to sit down; she avoided turning her back on him; she would not be drawn on various other peripheral matters on which he wanted to digress. She left him, still sensing a terrible and disturbing danger that stayed with her all that day. She felt relief not only in leaving him, but in having another appointment in another town. Ten hours later, the man had hacked his wife to death in a back garden, and hung himself in a local wood. No one knows if he had anyone else in mind, though the police certainly thought so, which is why they immediately tried to make contact with my colleague long before his body was found.

A most revealing description of violence perpetrated against a social worker is provided by Green (1982):

> Three months ago I was attacked by one of my clients and beaten over the head, shoulder, back, arms and hands with a piece of firewood. The sudden unexpectedness of it made me feel absolutely shattered, disbelieving and frightened...I felt very sick and in pain and needed desperately to get back to where I felt safe...My world was no longer within my control but far outside it and a repeated desire was to curl up in bed in the foetal position and forget it had

even happened. The worst realisation and the thought that kept recurring was that someone disliked me enough actually to hit me that hard and to hurt me that much. (p.19)

Here the worker's honest and vivid account highlights a common social work trait: the extreme reluctance to believe that their clients can be abominally cruel to them and to each other. Add to this reluctance, the 'armchair casework morality', the desire for civilised chats, and the 'self-consciousness process of reasoning', and there you have the perfect recipe for social work paralysis in crisis situations. That paralysis will surely exacerbate the crisis and increase the risks for all participants.

A strong sense of realism is vitally important for social workers attempting crisis intervention, the belief that such ugly features of crises actually do exist. When a worker acquires this sense of realism, it becomes possible to contemplate the necessity of having power authority and control, and the will and ability to use them. But what precisely do these terms mean, and what are the crisis circumstances which both demand and justify their use?

Power, authority and control in crisis intervention

Source and use

There are various forms of *power*. The worker has the power to provide financial and material aid in crisis situations. He has statutory powers, compelling him to act for the purpose of care and protection of clients. Such powers enable him to remove individuals from the crisis. Invoking these should be a last resort; indeed, the primary purpose of intervention is to avoid compulsory removal of clients if it is not in that clients' interest to be removed. The worker will be aided in that particular endeavour by exercising an entirely different kind of power; the power to establish himself in a position of influence and control at the very heart of the crisis without becoming dangerously identified with either side of the conflict. Techniques give him that power; for instance, the ability to deflate the initial anger and hostility by humour or ome other diversionary tactic; conveying both in words and gesture that he is not really a threat to anybody, that he is there primarily to find out about the crisis; exploiting space and seating to increase the impact of his presence upon all the crisis participants. Such tactics will quickly establish the worker as the necessary leader of the group, affording him additional power to direct proceedings as he sees fit.

The workers' *authority* in crisis should have three main sources. First, an authority by virtue of the request made to him to solve the crisis. Other agencies and crisis participants will hope and/or expect him to solve it, and will therefore be willing to some extent to recognise and respond to the directives which the worker is prepared to give. Secondly, the worker's professional training, experience, and statutory powers should give him an immense authority in the eyes of crisis clients and most of the crisis participants. The worker must be prepared therefore to demonstrate that authority in word and deed. Thirdly, the worker confirms and increases his status of authority by the exercise of his power and by the application of the techniques which bring about quick and dramatic changes in the atmosphere and course of the crisis.

The worker's obligation to *control* a crisis situation is determined by the loss of control and subsequent panic felt by the crisis participants. It is that sense of a loss of control which often compels the participants and other professionals to plead for social work intervention. If the worker decides he should intervene, then he must be prepared to exercise control. If the crisis arena is too vast in terms of numbers of participants and space, the worker must try to reduce it to manageable proportions. He must retain that control until the crisis atmosphere is transformed, until some degree of order and mutual respect becomes manifest; above all, until the degree of suffering and distress has been drastically reduced. Then the worker can contemplate the clients' capacity for exercising that control themselves, and if he believes it possible, his strategy then should be 'marked by a progressive disengagement...and the removal of the boundary which has held the family and therapist together' (Walrond-Skinner, 1976, p.68).

Manipulation

Biestek (1961) defines manipulation as 'the activity of maneouvering the client to choose or decide modes of action in accordance with the case-workers judgement in such a way that the client is not aware of the process; or if he is aware of it, he feels 'moved about' against his will' (1961, p.107). Manipulation then is a means of both acquiring and exercising power. It is often necessary in crisis situations. When one crisis participant is inflicting unnecessary suffering on another, when there is a very real risk of physical danger to the worker, and when crisis participants are clamouring for the compulsory removal of a client, manipulation is a wholly justifiable technique that enables the worker to resist or put an end to such damaging processes. It is an art of diplomacy requiring great sensitivity, experience and confidence. But it is well worth cultivating, because, as we have seen in the case of Sheila, it is an effective means of rescuing individuals from the psychological and emotional cruelties which others may be inflicting upon them. As we have also seen in that case, the worker lacking in experience and confidence, may choose a more direct method of achieving the same goal. In that instance, such an alternative method was possible. But in some instances, the explosive atmosphere of crisis, its sense of panic and helplessness, the fanatical and violent conviction of some crisis participants, would make the honest and explicit request of the worker for them ιo do something 'against their will' quite futile. Social workers in these kinds of crisis situations therefore, must be willing and able to manipulate individuals into acting against their will, if such a will is inflicting suffering on weaker individuals all around, threatening a physical attack on the worker, or if it is posing a major stumbling-block in the intervention process. Indeed, it would be morally indefensible to tolerate the sight and sound of such suffering on some half-baked notion of 'armchair casework morality', formulated by individuals for whom the crisis scenarios of Sheila and the Moores were obviously inconceivable.

Statutory removal

So far, this text has both implicitly and explicitly been more concerned with crises in which pleas or demands for removal have been made. These crises constitute the greatest challenge to social workers, managers and trainers alike. A principal goal in this text is to advocate the kind of superior crisis training and preparation that will enable workers to deal effectively with the crisis without acceding to the demand for removal. But another harsh reality about crisis intervention is that some of these plea-for-removal crises will indeed – and should – end in removal. What then is the purpose of a massive intervention by a social worker, and is there still a moral defence for the use of power authority, control and manipulation? The answer is that such use in such cases may even be more necessary.

There are civilised and uncivilised circumstances in which the decision to remove someone is made, and in which the actual move takes place. The most obvious uncivilised method of ending such crises is violence, followed by police involvement and prosecution. The consequences for personal relationships, social status, and the emotional life of children can be disastrous. When a social worker recognises those 'malignant irreversible trends towards the break up of family' (Ackerman, 1966) or merely believes that a temporary removal is in everyone's interests, he should try to help the crisis participants reach that same conclusion. But feelings are more important than consensus; just as in many crises revolving around custody and access between a child and its warring parents, the social worker must aim to minimise feelings of triumph and vindication on the one side, and defeat and humiliation on the other. He cannot abolish such feelings in a crisis, but he can attempt to enlighten the participants as to how destructive such feelings are for the long-term future of the client and particularly the children of clients. If he cannot minimise the expression of such feelings in that open and honest way, and if he believes that some individual(s) present are being emotionally harmed by such negative and destructive feelings, he is morally justified in attempting to minimise and control them by manipulation. But not just because of the harm of the moment. Such feelings will ensure the worst possible circumstances for removal, and generate worse feelings at the actual point of departure, for example, expressions of hatred, threats and counter threats, possible violence, thereby lengthening the time (if not indeed making it impossible) for a return and reconciliation.

Whether one is thinking in terms of enabling the client to stay, or removing the client, there is a fundamental point about crisis intervention that should never be forgotten. The intervention and its success or failure is a crucially important foundation upon which many of the clients and their families' future thoughts, words and actions may be based. The objective therefore must be to achieve the maximum civilising impact upon the uncivilised chaotic crisis and its suffering participants. To suggest that power, authority, control and manipulation, may help to make such an impact, may sound paradoxical: but in my recorded experiences of 'civilising' by 'manipulation', that is, enabling families and groups to withdraw from the brink of the statutory removals they are all clamouring for, I have become convinced that it is a paradox worth cultivating.

Impediments in training for crisis intervention

The 'oppressed', 'innocent' client!

Dismantling the system, power, authority, control, manipulation, directing the crisis...what kind of language is this? What can it mean? It surely has nothing to do with social work. Few social work textbooks and social work trainers have found time for such seemingly unsocial work attitudes and actions. But then, it has already been established beyond doubt that literature and training have ignored the whole field of crisis intervention in deprived communities and dismembered families, relying instead on periodical regurgitation of largely irrelevant classical literature. This is a little ironical, because those same classical crisis pioneers, had no qualms at all about their own power and authority and the use of it in controlling the crisis situation. Pittman *et al.* (1971) writes of 'the therapist subtly conveying great confidence in his ability to handle the immediate situation' (p.263).

In Chapter 6, it was suggested that social work students have not been encouraged to explore their own moral vulnerability in crisis situations, or, to be more precise, how some characteristics of the crisis can provoke fear in them and lead to acts of stupidity, cowardice and immorality, with damaging consequences for the client. But it also seems to me that social work students have been actively discouraged from exploring the immorality of clients themselves, their psychological and physical cruelty towards their weakest members; their abuse of their own power and authority, their lies and deceptions, their game-playing and vanity, their downright brutishness realistically observed by Jordan and Packman (1978). These unpleasant features of character are all likely ingredients in the crisis melting pot, and any social worker who does not acknowledge them is unlikely to be able to minimise their destructive impact in a crisis.

Why is it that British social work training courses have consistently projected an insulting, condescending and unvarying image of an 'oppressed' and 'innocent' client? What particular standpoint or conviction gives rise to this view? What is its relevance to the specific task of training for crisis intervention?

There appear to be at least three origins of the view. The first is one that has already been examined, namely, the 'armchair casework morality' based on the acute middle-class sensitivity towards the imbalance of power between a professional, educated, articulate worker, and a deprived inarticulate client; secondly, a conviction that because of clients', deprivations and their inability to articulate, social workers have tended to define clients' problems in their (the social worker's) own terms (Jordan, 1972). This is a criticism that has often been levelled at family therapists in particular. Consequently, it has provoked a strong reaction in many trainers, which, whilst it seeks to uphold the clients' rights to present and define problems in their own terms, it has nevertheless reinforced social workers' perceptions of clients as 'innocent', 'oppressed' people. Thirdly, the idealogical and political commitments in social work training have constructed perspectives from which it is impossible to recognise the harsh realities and ugliest features of crisis, and impossible also to consider individual clients and families except within the perceived context of a rotten social and political system, in which, it is believed, lies the cause of all client problems:

> ...when problems come to be seen as substantially or inherently structural, the action directed towards individuals comes to be seen as ineffective, and in so far as it does alleviate problems, it is supportive of the very system which causes them. (Wilding, 1982 p. 80)

All these convictions have given rise to an unhealthy criticism of welfare professionalism in general, and some aspects of social work in particular. The acquisition of expertese, practical skills, and techniques, is frowned upon, presumably because it is perceived as the means by which middle-class social workers can control, or impose their will, upon downtrodden clients. Jordan and Packman (1978) display great insight in the matter of social workers working with violent families, but, typical of many social work trainers, they shy away from the responsibility of training social workers in the techniques and skills that enable them to intervene effectively with such families. In a later publication Jordan (1984) declares his anti-expertise philosophy more bluntly. He dismisses the 'highly subtle and clever form of technical manipulation' (p.14) which social workers might acquire. He argues that that is not what social work is about; it is fundamentally 'a flexible way of negotiating outcomes over very difficult and complex issues' (p.14). Wilding (1980) celebrates the fact that social work expertise does not really amount to anything regarding positive changes in clients: 'What can only be immensely encouraging to those concerned for individual freedom and the life of the spirit, is our failure as a society to find any effective way of changing people' (p.47). Whan (1983) actually seems to scorn the worker's expertise and questions the source of moral authority for its use. He criticises systems and cybernetics theory which underpin much family therapy practice. He equates this knowledge and the acquired family therapy skills and competence with scientific rationalism. He claims that this trend towards scientific rationalism, which he also identifies in behaviourism, leads to a casting off of personal qualities such as 'intuition, charisma and concern'. He is particularly critical of manipulative techniques, and the 'instrumental' application of knowledge: both of which he refers to as 'calculizing' of human nature. His highly critical treatise has attracted sufficient attention to quote him more fully:

> Technique allows one to conceive of and act within the working relationship manipulatively. For a calculus of human nature reconstitutes the subjective and historical being of the client as an object...We define another human being in terms of it having the properties of an object; in terms of its supposed typicality. Such a calculus based on objectivistic regularities promises prediction or probability, and therefore control...To imitate the scientific methods lend a confirmation to the helping professions and a believing society of the essential rightness of how they deal with human problems. Through this kind of rationalism, and its reflective style of analytic decomposition, the resistances of the others' presence are subdued and explained away under the sway of usefulness and utility. In so far as the other is persuaded of this reifying calculus of his being, he is denied reflective access to his own being as a person; for this brand of scientific rationalism dehumanises the scope of self reflection. (p.328)

Implications for clients in crisis

What do these political, moral and philosophical convictions and the clear anti-expertise, anti-authority stance to which they have led, contribute towards the preparation of students who will very soon find themselves in the midst of chaotic, panic-stricken, highly conflictual crises, and who will bear the responsibility of doing something about them? A parallel question must be: what do clients who are suffering distress, panic, or physical injury hope for or expect from a worker to whom they cry out for help? The fact is that families in crisis very much need expert help. They also need the worker to be knowledgeable and experienced, confident, authoritive, and willing to lead and control within the crisis situation. Here is an old social work hand (unfortunately considered too old-fashioned and out of date by many of the new breed of trainers who replaced her in the sixties and seventies) speaking on the topic of 'Authority in Social Work':

> Authority as used here does not mean domination or wilful impositions. It conveys rather the meaning of carrying those rights and powers that are inherent in special knowledge and are vested in special functions. Sometimes in their zeal to affirm the client's own rights and powers (and perhaps in their valid humility) caseworkers have spoken and acted as though to deny that they have any experience or knowledge of greater usefulness than that of the client himself. To a person who feels helpless, this is indeed a sorry kind of equality. A person in need of help seeks someone who has the authority of knowledge and skill to help him; he goes to someone who knows more or is better able than himself, and it is the clients' very assumption that the caseworker carries this authority which infuses the relationship with safety and security and strengthens his response to guidance. (Perlman, 1957, p.69)

What is so depressingly common in those anti-social work expertise statements and convictions is an apparent blindness to the suffering of the moment which is at the heart of Perlman's concern. So too is it the major preoccupation of Kahn and Earle (1982), two psychiatrists who should be congratulated for at least giving their text on crisis and crisis intervention, the most realistic and meaningful title: *'The Cry for Help and the Professional Response'*. There is a strong impression given in the moral indignation of radical social work literature, of the writers standing a million light years away from the intense human suffering in many of the crises we have been discussing. Their contributions, however well-meaning, seem to be nothing more than political and philosophical exercises, steeped in a purely elitest jargon: ironically, displaying the same type of form content and tone which I have criticised in classical crisis literature, ensuring that neither they nor their readers gain any sense of the drama, passion and pain of crises which social workers daily have to face.

Conclusion

Crisis intervention is and must be action-orientated, for the simple reason that crises are nearly always action-manifested. The more time spent in intellectualising on the moral, political, philosophical and sociological dimensions of social work or even on the specific topic of crisis intervention itself, the less time is spent on acquiring the necessary skill and technique for effective crisis work. Of course the former is a vitally important component of any social work course; but its prevalence in social work training to the exclusion of the latter ensures that thousands of students leave social work courses wholly ill-equipped for the crisis tasks that lie ahead. If such unfortunate students could be denied crisis work it would not matter all that much, but no such quiet life awaits them in a social services office. Consequently, when they are plunged into the chaos, panic and cruelty of crisis they may find it: 'produces a turmoil of conflicting and confused feelings, which fixes the worker into a petrified stance, like a rabbit caught at night in the headlights of a car, impotent, with that peculiar impotence which brings about its own demise' (Moore, 1982, p.18). There is nothing that exposes the inadequacy of social work crisis training and the gaping cultural and class divide as much as the sight of a lone middle-class social worker frightened and paralysed by their first contact with the harsh realities of crises: no time for reflection; no support from a colleague; no resort to intellectual meanderings or verbal gymnastics or interminable moralising; no retreat, no escape. . . and God help the client!

Thankfully, there are some signs of an emerging sense of realism in social work training that will help to move us far on from the nonsensical orientations of the sixties and early seventies which have left many workers so ill-prepared for various crises tasks. Davies' lengthy chapter on 'The Power of the Social Worker' (1981) is eminently sensible and realistic, echoing similar convictions of Perlman, Timms (1964), Rapoport (1971), Younghusband (1967) and Pinker (1982). It is to be hoped that the wisdom and insight of social work educators like these, largely rejected by many lecturers and students during social work's anti-authority mayhem before and after Seebohm, will once again assume the prominence in training it deserves.

9

Social Services: the Organisational Context

Introduction: model enterprises and all that

Readers are not going to be subjected now to a string of 'management must...' recommendations; those naively optimistic and self-righteous calls for dramatic changes at every level of the social services hierarchy. Readers will also be spared descriptions of those splendid multidisciplinary crisis intervention teams of London and New York, with the accompanying message for management: 'This Is How It Should Be'. Like most social workers, I work in one of those small area offices that is neither inner city nor rurally isolated. There are no spectacular enterprises in Selby; there is no multidisciplinary crisis-specialising team, nor is there ever likely to be. There are no Caplans, nor Scotts, nor Langsleys, nor Rapoports; there are no crisis centres of excellence in nearby towns, there are no readily available video-recording facilities (except if one is prepared to do a sixty minutues choc-a-bloc journey to the divisional office in York to collect it). And finally, there is not even an Emergency duty team in the whole of North Yorkshire, nor an intake system in Selby itself.

There is little point in seeking out the numerous and genuine reasons for this state of affairs, and, even less, in moaning about it; it is the norm rather than the exception throughout the country. But no management should interpret such a view as them being let off the hook, in regard to their responsibilities for an effective crisis service. On the contrary, the organisational and management contexts can have a profound influence on how social workers respond to crisis situations. This chapter will explore the minimum changes required to ensure that that influence is a positive one; first, at the supervisory — which usually means team-leader middle-management — level and then within senior management and the department as a whole.

Crisis intervention: the challenge for management

A wealth of experience

Social Services, in their very brief life span, have acquired more experience of crisis situations than any other agency during that same period. They deal with a far greater variety of crises, often including those in which fundamental human rights are under threat. They are persistently called upon by much longer established, more prestigious agencies, to solve crises which the latter cannot solve themselves. The first major task for management therefore, is simply to start believing this undeniable fact; and to begin to act in such a way as to make it obvious to the staff they manage and the public they serve. Crisis training in social work courses is appallingly inadequate, and the importance of engendering a feeling of confidence on the matter within social services departments themselves, cannot be overestimated.

Establishing the facts

The crisis challenge in terms of actual numbers and categories of crises, and the resources to deal with them, will vary enormously from area to area. Facts have to be established. Every crisis referral over a given period of time should be scrutinised. What is the most common type of crisis for that team in that area? Which have been the most difficult in terms of complexity, duration, expense and statutory involvement and consequence? A hierarchy of crises will emerge, covering a certain period, and it may look something like this:

No. of referrals	*Type of crisis*
19	Friends, neighbours, GP, relatives, etc., requesting/demanding that elderly confused persons be admitted into care.

18	Adolescents – parental conflict (over 70% step-parents): Demands/plea for removal.
17	Wife battering, request for protection and shelter
14	Child abuse/family crisis
11	Request for compulsory Admission into Psychiatric hospital
7	Homelessness
5	Destitution

It is quite clear from this list that the elderly confused pose a considerable crisis challenge during the chosen period. But not just in terms of numbers; we have seen that such crises have enormous social, moral and statutory implications (see Chapter 5). Having established this order of crises, team leaders should then examine how the team members are responding. Is there consistency of approach, philosophy, and goal? Are there vast differences in the levels of knowledge and confidence in dealing with such crisis, in the skills and techniques used; in the impacts and outcomes of intervention? (The worst kind of managerial resistance to simple, basis research like this takes the form of: 'every crisis situation is different and so is every social worker'). To isolate a particular crisis category like this, is not meant to exclude various other less pressing types of crises; social services will as always be expected to respond and will to some extent have to pretend to respond well to every conceivable form of crisis! Rather, it is meant to achieve a collective awareness of where the greatest crisis challenge to the team lies, and, subsequently, to gain a consensus and willingness on the part of team members, to meet that challenge in a more disciplined knowledgeable and effective way. If a team begins the exercise by concentrating on only one – the most common, the most difficult – type of crisis, there will be a greater chance of success, and there will be many advantageous spin-offs for tackling other categories.

Social workers' limitations for crisis work

The crisis challenge cannot be met by some young inexperienced social workers who have a near phobic fear of many different types of crisis situations. The origins of the fear as we have seen, may lie in inadequate social work training, in which case, excellent supervision can do something about it. But fear and consequential incompetence may have more fundamental root causes, such as an upbringing and temperament totally alien to, and seriously threatened by, the atmosphere of panic, violence, and unpredictability of many of the crises we have been discussing. (Jordan and Packman, 1978, is an excellent guide on this matter.) There is no cause for surprise here. Clark's (1971) rare piece of research on how social workers respond to mental illness crises indicates the extent of the problem. This research was carried out in an inner London borough and was confined to an emergency duty team, a location and provision in which one would normally expect to find crisis expertise and competence. On the contrary, Clark found not a single worker enthusiastic about the crisis task. Worst of all, he could not find a worker who viewed the crisis as a potentially therapeutic situation. He concluded: 'social workers dislike the emergency situation...many crises remained unresolved...' (p.36).

Respecting and responding to the worker's limitations

It is nothing less than irresponsible and wholly immoral on the part of management in general and team leaders in particular to allow such staff to inflict their genuine distaste of crisis and their consequential fear and incompetence, upon crisis participants, particularly when there has been the request or demand for invoking statutory powers as a means of resolving the crisis. Everyone knows that that kind of immorality was rampant in the immediate post-Seebohm years, and that incalculable damage was the inevitable result for literally thousands of clients. Team leaders are not being asked to make dramatic changes here; they simply need to establish who such workers are, and to tactfully enable them to accept that this aspect of personality, this background, this genuine fear and distaste of crisis work will be respected. It should not be too difficult. Unlike many in social work training, most team leaders will have had a certain amount of crisis experience themselves. They may well identify with such workers, and they should not attempt to conceal their own crisis shortcomings. A team leader in Selby, to his credit, once declared his profound reluctance to involve himself in crises of the mentally ill; that did not minimise his responsibility and authority to determine precisely who should deal with these crises; on the contrary, a team leader who has this honesty and humility is likely to be a more accurate assessor of the potentialities and vulnerabilities in others, and respected more for it.

Crisis intervention and staff supervision

Knowledge: the crisis context

Having established the most pressing crisis problem upon which to concentrate, and having unburdened some team members of the awful prospect of dealing with those crises, the team leader then has an opportunity of monitoring the development of individual crisis competence and the team's collective impact upon that particular crisis category. Team leaders too should find the crisis self-awareness frameworks in Chapter 6 helpful. But their principal responsibility is to ensure the worker has every opportunity to acquire both knowledge and skill in order that they may make the maximum contribution towards the team's crisis service to the particular and recurring crisis problem. Acquiring knowledge does not mean allowing time off for browsing in the library; team members will find little at all there on crisis intervention in social services; but it does mean encouraging the worker to research every conceivable aspect of the crisis, and its family, social and environmental contexts. The aim should be to elicit pattern, process and meaning from it. With this kind of understanding, workers will also learn of those features of the crisis which pose the greatest challenge to them. It may well be the entry point, joining the crisis system; it may be dealing with violence or potential violence; or it may be handling a large group. When the problem is identified the team leader has a major responsibility to help the worker overcome it. The most accurate and detailed recording of experiences in which this problem manifests itself, is imperative. Let us say for example that a worker finds it extremely difficult – as most workers do – to deal with a large group of persons in a crisis situation. A detailed recording of a case in point and a thorough joint analysis by team leader and worker may reveal – most likely will reveal – that it is not so much the large group as that its members are spread all over the place, agitated, noisy, tense, constantly moving about, behind the worker, in front of him, walking in and out. What social worker would not be discomfited by that spectacle? As Moore (1982) implies, most social workers would try to 'act' their way through such a crisis. They detest themselves being seen unruffled and uncertain. They may be encouraged in this attitude by an entirely unhelpful kind of supervision, in which the team leader also engages in an act, pretending that such a group is indeed manageable, and this is what you should be saying to them. Such dangerous nonsense is the surest guarantee of a worker's inability to gain a grip on the crisis proceedings. Supervisors should advise their workers not to attempt to manage such a group. As has already been demonstrated, there are subtle ways of reducing it. Team leaders should know of the style, temperament and experience which will determine which is the more appropriate way for each worker, the way of least risk and probable success. But the principle remains: social workers must seek an environment of people and circumstances that is both manageable and reasonable as a basis for exploring the crisis and intervening effectively. If the group, and in particular the most influential person in it, does not respond, then the worker should be given every support and encouragement by the team leader to make a temporary withdrawal from the crisis situation. My experiences tell me however, that behind all the chaos and noise of crisis, participants are fully aware of the implications and risks to their own interests, should they sustain an atmosphere which makes it impossible for the worker to continue.

Recording: a crucial learning tool

All the stages of the intervention should be subjected to the same detailed scrutiny, and must primarily and initially depend upon the worker's detailed recording of experiences. This is a crucial point and supervisors must insist on it. The temptation to walk away from an emotionally draining and threatening crisis, to seek solace amongst friends always more than willing to oblige, is difficult to resist. But the longer one waits to recover, the more quickly memories of vitally significant thoughts, feelings and actions will fade. A mere ten minutes immediately after the crisis is all that is needed to record or to write just single words and phrases as subject headings, encapsulating not-to-be-forgotten moments in the drama: for example, the moment when a father cried and the worker felt helpless; or the moment when one realises there is an alliance between certain crisis participants as impregnable as it was destructive; or the most uncomfortable realisation that one's actions are on behalf of one's (harrassed) self rather than the client.

Supervision: ethical considerations

Crisis intervention in social services is fraught with risks of unprincipled, unprofessional conduct by social workers. There are two almost opposite kinds of immorality which might be manifest: the first stems from an inability to face up to certain unpleasant features of the crisis situations, which then leads to damaging reactions enabling the worker to avoid that responsibility; the second is the misuse of authority, knowledge and technique in the unnecessary control and manipulation of clients. Certain characteristics of crisis situations in the homes and localities of social work clients are conducive to both of these opposing moral vulnerabilities: a family or social culture characterised by violence, exceptionally high noise levels, constant bickerings and walk-outs, may on occasions simply overwhelm the worker, compelling him to escape by any unprincipled tactic he may think of; on the other hand, the fear and helplessness of clients in crisis, their general lack of sophistication, their inability to articulate, can make them surrender 'any last vestige of independance and influence they may have possessed' to the manipulative control of the worker (O'Hagan, 1984).

To speak bluntly, the team leader's task here is to accompany the worker along the crisis tightrope, minimising the risk of him tumbling head over heels into the feebleness and cowardice on one side, and the arrogant self-styled ominipotence on the other. It is debatable which is the greater evil, though some may have no doubt when they listen to this supposedly prominent figure in the family therapy movement: 'I decided I was going to drive the mother mad if that was necessary to take responsibility for her' (Skynner, 1979, p.16). Thankfully social workers are unlikely to indulge in this kind of megalomania. The persistent disciplined use of the self-exploration frameworks in Chapter 6, by worker and supervisor combined, will help one avoid either of these opposite and dangerous vulnerabilities.

Team leaders carry an enormous burden of responsibility for effective principle-based crisis intervention by their members, not just because of the multiple complexities of the crisis task, but also because of the consequences of incompetence on client and social worker alike, and ultimately on the team itself. Social work teams are admirably kind and supportive to their members in distress, but that instinctive rallying and its accompanying defensive manouevres against the crisis world outside is not really conducive to an objective and rigorous examination of the quality of intervention offered to the client. In the long term , the latter is probably of greater service to the worker in question than the former, and team leaders in particular should be equal to the task.

Senior management and crisis intervention

Accepting the realities

The first task for senior management is acceptance of some basic realities which have been repeatedly emphasised in this text; first, that as social services departments develop and establish themselves in the community, members of the public and other agencies (particularly the police) will increasingly refer crises to them; secondly, that the plea-for-removal of the elderly confused and of the troublesome step-child (adolescents) type of crises will inevitably rise as a consequence of social and demographic trends over which social services departments have no control; thirdly, that if, for sound financial or other sensible reasons, they cannot contemplate the establishment of some high-powered multidisciplinary crisis team to deal with a particular category of crisis, they are capable nevertheless, of influencing the level of crisis competence on the part of individual social workers; fourthly, that there is a powerful economic incentive as well as a moral obligation to attempt to raise that level of crisis competence. When these realities are accepted by senior managers, they will be more disposed to address themselves to the task of helping individual social workers to intervene in crises more effectively. They may be surprised to learn just how influential they could be, for example, in the following areas: supervision, crisis principles, and inter-agency co-operation.

Supervision: the task for senior management

Social workers involved in crisis work, particularly family crisis, need a very reliable, competent and experienced supervisor. Most social workers do not have any choice in this matter. It is usually the team leader who supervises all the team members. There are very few team leaders experienced and competent in family crisis work, even less with a crisis training and theoretical knowledge-base. Consequently, their supervision of social workers embroiled in crises lacks confidence and conviction. Social workers know it.

Senior management has two options here. It can leave the existing situation as it is and try to ensure that all future team leaders have sufficient crisis experience and knowledge which can encourage and reassure team members as they are about to engage in crisis work. The other option is much more radical, and may be opposed ironically by team members and social workers alike. It is the logical extension of Jordan and Packman's (1978) suggestion of a 'reservoir of experienced workers'; it is to designate those team members who are the most experienced and knowledgeable crisis interventionists, as the team's crisis supervisors for those categories of crisis which pose the greatest challenge to the team, in terms of (a) risks; (b) the clamour for invoking statutory power; and (c) the long-term consequences for worker, clients and department. Team leaders may oppose such a move, which they are likely to interpret as a diminition of their authority and power. And some social workers may be less than enthusiastic, expressing a gut reaction prevalent in the profession against any form of elitism, against anyone volunteering their crisis expertise and experience to the service of the team. This 'structural' and 'personal' reluctance on the part of leader and team members precludes the possibility of a speedy and whole-hearted implimentation of the idea. But if senior management was to declare it official policy, and was prepared to monitor its development, scrutinising the course of events when, for example, plea-for-removal crisis referrals are made, then teams as a whole would be more receptive.

Crisis policies compatible with crisis principles

If a social worker on duty or on stand-by intervenes successfully in a crisis over a prolonged period of hours, there are likely to have been a number of developments. First, social worker and clients will have become thoroughly familiar with and trusting of each other. Secondly, all the initial fears and apprehensions and misperceptions which the client(s) had about social services involvement will have been allayed and corrected. Thirdly, the client(s) will be heavily dependent upon the worker, and apprehensive about the worker's departure. They will seek reassurance that the worker will return, or can be easily contacted.

From similar observations, the crisis pioneers of forty years ago laid down the principle – and have been emphasising its importance ever since – that if a worker is going to embroil himself in crisis with a particular individual or family, he must be available to return to them soon and frequently at any time during the immediate post-crisis period. It seems a most logical principle. Crises are seldom solved by a single intervention. The worker knows that it is successful only in that it defuses the crisis and creates at atmosphere of relative calm which has to be sustained and strengthened by further visits, at least one within the following twenty-four hours. The success of the initial intervention will have depended upon many things, not least upon the skill and sensitivity to relate (positively) to each of the crisis participants. As we have seen, this is a complex operation, which, when completed, will underpin all subsequent strategies for dealing with the crisis.

This crisis principle, which places such emphasis upon familiarity and availability between worker and client(s), is widely ignored by social workers in social services departments. The common distaste of many kinds of crises is well served by duty, standby, and EDT systems, in which workers keep an eager eye on the clock, knowing that if they can survive until a certain time they can hand the crisis over to somebody else. Clearly there is a need for a policy compatible with the principle. Families in crisis do not want nor should they need to be subjected once again to the hazardous business of getting to know and trust another social worker. The existing system, in which geographical boundaries are jealously guarded yet allow the occasional duty foray into some family crisis, acts against the principle in another way, having profound repercussions for the quality of crisis service. It discourages social workers from thinking that the crisis resolution is their responsibility — it is really that of the worker or team normally covering the area! Consequently, the duty or standby officer may approach the task with neither enthusiasm nor determination to get too involved, thereby re-affirming the natural distaste of crisis work and the belief that nothing can be done in any case. This is particularly the result when duty or standby officers are those totally unsuited in temperament, upbringing and lack of training for crisis work.

Is this the best that senior management can offer? I suggest not. Senior management should declare that in the field of crisis intervention, factors like geographical boundaries and shift duration need not be sacrosanct, and that team leaders in particular, allow workers who have intervened successfully when the initial crisis referral was made, to continue with the good work, in line with a sound principle. (It would be naive to expect the wholesale implementation of a crisis policy incorporating a principle that probably very few in management are aware of, but it would be a major leap forward if those social workers thoroughly familiar with it in theory could be allowed to practice it!).

Other agencies' perceptions of crisis intervention in social services

The third task for management is a PR exercise directed at the public at large, but more specifically at those agencies with whom social services need to work in harmony on a multiplicity of social ills. Good crisis intervention not only requires courage, integrity, sensitivity and numerous skills and techniques, but also the confidence and authority to pursue a course of action contrary to the wishes and demands of powerful individuals and agencies. Management must first of all believe that social workers, by virtue of their community base, professional training, personal qualities, and values and principles which the profession espouses, do at least have the potential for providing a crisis service far superior to that offered by the neighbours, GPs, health visitors, and so on, who continually request social workers to solve crises. Then management should make it absolutely clear that, whilst the department will respond promptly to various categories of crisis, that response is not likely to take the form envisaged by the referrer.

The social and demographic trends which make an increase in crisis referral rates inevitable, are certain to highlight the ethical and philosophical differences which lie behind the contrasting approaches to crises, by social workers and other agency professionals. The latter, more influenced by the crisis atmosphere than perhaps they would admit, seek simple, immediate solutions, which often mean statutory powers and residential care. Social workers have learnt to live with that kind of pressure, but the complex and risky task of crisis intervention would be greatly assisted without it. Senior managers are well placed to take an initiative for this purpose. In the numerous meetings and contacts with their counterparts in other agencies, they have an opportunity to at least explain the social work perspective of crisis. They must, when a suitable case arises, demonstrate that a worker's refusal to 'solve' a crisis by the statutory removal which they are demanding, is no more passing aberration; that it will – and why it should – increasingly become the rule rather than the exception; that in many of these plea-for-removal crisis referrals, the greatest challenge for the worker, and the focal point of their efforts will lie somewhere in the midst of those professionals and lay persons clamouring for removal, rather than in the client at the centre of the crisis. Whether this educative process will filter through to make any impact upon teachers, health visitors, and GPs, is another matter; but from the social worker's point of view, it can only be reassuring to know that their own senior management is aware of these additional pressures; more importantly, that in spirit at least they stand by the worker in resisting them, and above all, that senior management itself will not succumb to the same when the worker's back is turned. Many a social worker will know that the latter occurance is not all that rare.

Conclusion

Management generally, therefore, does have an important role to play in sustaining the level of crisis competence acquired by individual social workers. No fundamental, structural or financially crippling changes have been demanded in this chapter; no new group or interminable committee mechanisms, no spectacular innovations. An appreciation of crisis intervention as a discipline in its own right is called for, and an acknowledgement of how often social workers face a variety of crisis situations alone, in both old and new cases. Thereafter, the chapter has provided commonsensical suggestions which need threaten no one, except those who have been deluding themselves that an excellent social services crisis provision already exists. Far be it for a mere field worker to 'instruct' management, but there are historical facts and significant trends to emerge from the evolution of crisis intervention in social services, which need to be stressed repeatedly, to management in particular and to the profession as a whole:

1. The Maria Colwell report (1974) and all subsequent enquiries (HMSO 1982) clearly indicate the lack of skill, knowledge and confidence which existed when the numerous crises in these cases erupted. The subsequent deteriorations in terms of relationships between clients and departments were to a large extent a direct consequence of bad crisis intervention at various stages in the course of events.

2. 'Crisis' is the context in which the vast majority of residential placements are made – the crises of the elderly, the mentally ill, battered wives, abused children, and so on. Ten years after Maria Colwell, at which time social workers were criticised for their inaction, they are now hounded by journalists, attacked by pressure groups, and laughed at in the popular arts, because of a widespread perception of their abuse of statutory powers by the removal of clients at the slightest provocation or whim. Significant figures within the profession actually strengthen such perceptions (Jordan, 1981), more seriously alleging that workers invariably direct care proceedings against the poorest multi-problem families. This latter cheap debating point – which social workers cannot really contest – and its impact upon public perceptions, should compel management to scrutinise the crisis contexts of residential placements; not just to be able to argue that residential care is a vitally important and effective contingency resource for crisis work, but more importantly, that skilled, experienced crisis practitioners have been able to avoid the inappropriate and damaging use of that resource.

The principle of crisis intervention as a beginning rather than an end is particularly pertinent to management. If it is wrongly seen as an 'end', this in reality usually means a 'beginning'; some drastic solution (like residential care) that can cost the department dearly, in terms of the emotional and physical investment by individual social workers, and the actual financial cost to the department for providing long-term residential care, solicitor's fees,worker's time, expenses, and so on. If – as it should be – crisis intervention is seen as a 'beginning' that ideally should mean an 'end', the end of panic, helplessness and despair, a recognition of the therapeutic potential which the crisis situation offers; the conviction that the department, in the person of the social worker, can exploit that potential, and enable the client to emerge from the crisis far better equipped in terms of insight, tolerance and self-confidence, to make long-term involvement unnecessary.

To summarise all this in a couple of words soothingly comprehensible to the ears of managers and social services committees alike; an effective grass roots crisis intervention service is infinitely *cheaper* and *better*.

10

Crisis Intervention

But whose crisis?

16 July, 1984; location: a North Yorkshire village

Thy said it most certainly was a crisis. Old Sam had 'flipped his lid' again. The homehelp, a former mental health nurse, literally pleaded with her senior to get something done. Mrs Murray next door could not take any more. Mrs Jones, a life-long neighbour and friend of Sam had been wakened three times the previous night by his knocking on the door. Big sergeant McGill complained too, said two of his officers had been called out because there was Sam wandering in the dead hour of night with no trousers on; Dr Harvey bluntley asked how 'dead' Sam would have to be before we made a move; he had left him an hour ago, totally paralytic and sick having consumed half a bottle of whisky; now, said Dr Harvey, he was gulping down that peculiar mixture of vinegar and sugar, which, in phases like this, he simply could not resist. And this was a very sudden phase, because Sam had been discharged from the psychiatric ward no more than two weeks ago. The consultant was saying a very definite 'no' to the request for readmission.

I was not keen about this referral. I knew Sam quite well. I had dealt with a number of similar crises previously. Sam had a compulsive need to grip people like a vice when he was speaking to them. His grip often hurt me, and occasionally frightened me. A long time ago, I ignored the warnings of a GP and family members about the dangerousness of a young very strong psychotic person. At one point in the interview, without any hint at all, he suddenly grabbed me by the throat. I have never forgotten the experience, nor totally lost the sense of his powerful grip. I do not like anyone to hold me in a vice-like grip, least of all a client who is mentally ill.

Mrs Murray was out when I arrived. So too was Mrs Jones. I knocked the doors of the next three houses. Only one resident, an elderly woman, was at home. She was aware of all the goings on with Sam, but she did not want to talk about it. She had her own problems, she said. I walked back to Sam's both disappointed and apprehensive; I always seek the assistance of a neighbour in making contact with the elderly confused.

The rotting door of Sam's tumble-down glass porch was open. I would have preferred it to be closed and locked. I shouted his name and some greeting, trying to sound both confident and calm. There was no reply. I entered the porch and tried the door of his living room. It too was unlocked, I opened it a little and shouted again; still no reply. I went inside, into the darkest most cluttered living room imaginable. Sam never really 'retired'; the tools of his cobbling trade littered the place, including the pure leather products of half-a-century ago, boots and shoes that today a months' salary could not buy. You could hardly move in Sam's living room, which was often the reason why I painfully tolerated his vice-like grip.

For a few moments I just stood there, grateful that Sam was not in my sight. But I was conscious of a time limit on this particular 'privilege'. I walked towards the tattered curtains that concealed the entrance to a narrow even darker winding staircase. The air was laden with the stench of urine and excrement. I looked up the staircase, and the thought of walking up there filled me with dread. I did not call out Sam's name. I did not want him to hear me. I did not want to see him. So I just stood there, at the bottom of the stairs, gazing up, becoming increasingly impotent with fear, and almost disbelieving of my impotence and fear. I suppose it was the realisation of a drift into total paralysis that eventually made me call out; it felt good. I did it again, louder this time; there was not a sound. I did not call out a third time; it seemed neither intelligent nor brave. I thought of Sam dying on his bed, and still I could not move. In fact it was precisely that thought that was immobilising me; that dying though he may be, his grip might be that much tighter, and that I would panic knowing I could never loosen his grip; worst of all was the thought that all this would take place in the trap of his tiny back bedroom, seemingly a million miles from the escape of his front door.

I could not stand these thoughts. I went back through the living room and out the front door, hoping I might see someone and they might accompany me up those ghastly stairs. But the village was desolate, and I felt no inclination to knock on any more doors. I felt like a fool and was sure I looked like one. I returned to the foot of the stairs, determinedly. I placed a foot on the first step and hesitated. That was the surest guarantee that my other foot was not going to reach the second step. I knew it, and retreated, deciding I must get a colleague to accompany me. I drove away, humiliated. About a mile from the village I stopped. I had to stop; the feelings of cowardice and stupidity and guilt were overwhelming me. After a few moments, I turned the car and went back. I hurried through the living room and up the winding stairs. There was another tattered and filthy curtain across the door of the bedroom. I pulled it aside and went in, my heart pounding and my knees trembling. There was Sam on his bed, sleeping soundly, his bare legs and bottom covered in excrement, and the empty half bottle of whisky at his side. There was no crisis here.

Self-exploration: the unending search

This was not the way I had intended finishing this book, but I am unaware of any incident or literary convention that would allow me to encapsulate one of its principle themes more effectively; that self-knowledge and self-awareness are the most valuable assets for crisis work. Had someone suggested that Monday morning, that I was likely to behave as I have described, I would have laughed at them. Six, seven, eight years ago, most certainly ten years ago, as the first chapter would indicate, I could easily accept I was as vulnerable as that; but 1984? No!

In the hours which followed, I spent a lot of time trying to analyse that vulnerability. Was it a phobia, developing from a horrible experience in the past? was it the environment, dark and foul? was it the silence, as deafening and disturbing as any violent family crisis? in retrospect, I am inclined to think that the principle cause was none of these; that it was more fundamentally professional pride and arrogance blinding me to the need for caution; a little humble contemplation of some difficulties I might have encountered besides the unpleasantness of Sam's grip, 'difficulties' lurking in my own heart and mind, for example. I have previously stressed the importance of a 'a little contemplation' before embarking upon crisis intervention, and when frantic referrals speak of ghastly rows, and ask or demand that a social worker gets out there pronto for the sake of some poor devil in the midst of it all, that is precisely what I do: sit and ponder for a while. But Sam, an old man alone, just the two of us – indeed as it turned out, just me alone, what kind of contemplation was necessary for that?

During the writing of this book I have naturally been much more aware of my responses in crisis situations. I honestly did believe at the outset, that I had all the experience and the authority to make some contribution to this particular field, and that I was fully justified in pointing out the shortcomings of managers and trainers alike for what I interpreted as their entirely inadequate responses to the crisis challenge. But the experience in Sam's living room has been only one of many during this last twelve months which have compelled me to scrutinise once again my own inadequacies; my own lack of training, knowledge, self-discipline and self-awareness. Of course, I have had more than ten years experience of crisis work in Selby; of course the subject fascinates me and I have spent many pleasant hours analysing and writing about it, and trying to improve on it. But there are no neat developmental progressive stages in the process; it does not easily lend itself to the analytical and compartmentalised certainties which the crisis pioneers were determined to impose upon it; and if we delude ourselves that we have succeeded in doing that, some entirely new crisis situation is sure to convince us otherwise, painfully so. That is no bad thing. There can be no end to the journey of self-exploration in crisis work. Occasionally, after some shocking and painful milestone, we may hope there is; but no sooner has it passed but we realise the inner strength which the pain itself has given us; experience, understanding, humility – the means by which we may if we choose, prepare a little more for our next crisis. I will prepare a little more for my next visit to Sam.

Crisis intervention : the real meaning

What is the point of crisis intervention? At a time when many social work writers and trainers are telling us that we should all be community workers, crisis intervention may be regarded as something of an anachronism. The laudable goal of the former is to bring about change in the existing local political and social structures and thereby enhance the quality of life in the community as a whole. This must surely be preferable to what might be perceived as a fleetingly brief intervention which can have no lasting positive impact. But the latter is not what crisis intervention is about. In crisis, clients will often make lightning decisions and embark upon a course of action which is profoundly more damaging in its effect than any environmental, social, economic or political force or structure surrounding them. Some may argue that it is precisely these structures and forces which pressurise the client into making such decisions. They should listen more to their clients, who will reveal that whatever oppressive force is bearing down upon them, they have a pride and an independent spirit, the manifestations of which are entirely unpredictable in a crisis situation. That is why Mary, one of umpteen clients I recall, endures phases of unmitigated guilt. Her son Tony spent the first eleven happy years of his life with his doting grandparents in Scotland. They did not know anything about social work or social workers. They gave the kid love and commitment, and he thrived, whilst his mother drifted from one marital hell to another, in Selby. Then during a home visit, a crisis developed between Mary and her parents; other family members became involved. The flaming rows which erupted were 'resolved' by Mary 'exercising her right' of taking her child with her, back to Selby. She paid dearly for that decision, and her son, now languishing in prison after six years of intermittent care, paid even more. Mary knows what happened. She blames no one but herself, and she would not understand anyone trying to convince her otherwise.

This idea of 'decision-making' is central in the evolution of crisis theories and crisis intervention services. The pioneers may have given up on the task of definition, but some of them at least were aware of the origins of the word: it is the Greek *krisis*, meaning quite literally a decision. The Chinese represent the word with the use of characters denoting both 'danger' and 'opportunity', two features of crisis which have figured prominently throughout this text. Combined, the Greek and the Chinese interpretations of the crisis concept do not take us any further in the task of definition, but the image they evoke, of *decision-making in conditions of both danger and opportunity* is as succinct and adequate an understanding of crisis and crisis intervention, as we ever are likely to find. It is particularly appropriate in the social services context, where, however overwhelmed we are by the extent of a client's poverty and deprivation, we know that those same clients are quite capable of and quite often do in crisis situations – decide on a course of action which will make their overall situation – marital, financial, social and psychological – infinitely worse.

There is nothing uncommon about clients like Mary making disastrous decisions in crisis situations. But this book is far more about social workers equipping themselves sufficiently to ensure that they are not a party to similar decisions; that they have the knowledge, skill and self-awareness to respond to the request for intervention in such a way as to enable clients to see that there are far more preferable alternatives. In no area of crisis work, is this more necessary than in plea-for-removal crises. It is tragic, when poor inarticulate clients, battered and bruised, disowned and stigmatised, decide upon a course of action that will prove to be disastrous for themselves and some innocent party around them. But what is it when educated professional people make equally disastrous decisions when caught up in a plea-for-removal crisis. The difference is of course, that clients have to live with the consequences of their action; social workers do not; their decisions can be shared; the major responsibility handed over to residential staff; the case transferred to a successor when one leaves; the client eventually forgotten about.

The emphasis throughout this book has been on the 'plea-for', rather than on the 'removal' itself. A social worker will and must on occasions consider removal as the most appropriate option in the crisis. But it is the impact of the 'plea', the clamour, the demand for removal, on the social worker and department alike, which has been our primary concern. Crisis intervention is not easy in such circumstances. As well as the possibility of being stampeded into making the wrong move, one also has the option of withdrawing. Of course it would be much more convenient to leave the crisis and return to the office base, to drink coffee and discuss with friendly colleagues,to decide not to tackle the problem until passions subside (when the crisis is over!), to arrange a series of interviews, to explore the history, to relate to the client, to ascertain mutual goals, to draw up a contract; this is definitely the organised, disciplined, professional, middle-class mind at work. In social work generally this is to be highly recommended; in crisis intervention it is often a middle-class cop out, as inexplicable and unhelpful to the client as it is irrelevant to the crisis processes.

Let no one then underestimate the essential and revolutionary goals of crisis intervention: to replace blind, ugly passion with enlightenment and tolerance, chaos and panic with order and safety, helplessness and despair with a sense of hope. Cynics may believe one seeks a miracle, and others may believe one seeks a permanent solution. (How boring and unnatural if such a replacement was to be permanent!) Crisis intervention merely seeks those kind of conditions in order to minimise the 'danger' in a crisis situation, preventing clients from being consumed by the panic of crisis, and eventually enabling them to *freely* make decisions about their own lives.

Bibliography

Ackerman, N.W. (1966) *Teaching the Troubled Family*, New York, Basic Books Inc.

Aguilera, D.C. and Messick, J.N. (1980) *Crisis Intervention: Theory and Methodology*, St Louis, Mosby.

Aponte, H.J. (1976) 'Underorganisation in the poor family', in Guerin, P.J. (ed.) *Family Therapy: Theory and Practice*, New York, Gardner Press.

Aponte, H.J. (1977) 'The Anatomy of a Therapist', in Papp, P. (ed.) *Family Therapy: Full Length Case Studies*, New York, Gardner Press, Inc.

Barclay, P.M. (1982) *Social Workers: Their Roles and Tasks*, London, Bedford Square Press.

British Association of Social Workers (1984) *Out of Hours Social Work*: Report of a BASW Research Study.

Bentovim, A., Gorell Barnes, G. and Cooklin, A. (eds) (1982) *Family Therapy: Complementary Frameworks of Theory and Practice* (2 vols), London, Academic Press.

Bertalanffy, L. von (1968) *General Systems Theory*, London, Allen Lane, Penguin Press.

Bertalanffy, L. von (1972) 'General Systems Theory - a critical review', in Beishon, J. and Peters, G. (eds) *Systems Behaviour*, Open University Press.

Biestek, F. (1961) *The Casework Relationship*, London, Unwin.

Bloch, S.A. (1973) *Techniques of Family Psychotherapy: A Primer*, New York, Grune & Stratton.

Boszormenyi-Nagy, I and Framo, J. (eds) (1965) *Intensive Family Therapy*, New York, Harper & Row.

Bott, E. (1971) 'Families in crisis', pp.17-30 in Sutherland, J.D. (ed.) *Towards Community Mental Health*, London, Tavistock.

Bott, E. (1976) 'Hospital and society', *British Journal of Medical Psychology*, 49,pp.97-140.

Buckle, J. (1981) *Intake Teams*, London, Tavistock.

Butler, A. and Pritchard, C. (1983) *Social Work and Mental Illness*, London, Macmillan.

Cade, B. (1980) 'Strategic therapy', *Journal of Family Therapy*, 2,pp.89-99.

Caplan, G. (1961) *A Community Approach to Mental Health*, London, Tavistock.

Caplan, G. (1964) *Principles of Preventative Psychiatry*. New York, Basic Books.

Clark, J. (1971) 'An analysis of crisis management by mental welfare officers', *The British Journal of Social Workers*, 1(1),pp.27-38.

Cooklin, A. (1979) 'A psychoanalytic framework for a systemic approach to family therapy', *Journal of Family Therapy*, 1,pp.153-166.

Corie, A. (1976) 'Intake: friend or foe?', *Social Work Today*, 6 (23),pp.10-12.

Coulshed, V. (1981) '"Engaging" in family therapy: problems for the inexperienced uninvited therapist', *Journal of Family Therapy*, 3,pp.51-8.

Dale, P. (1981) 'Family therapy and incomplete families', *Journal of Family Therapy*, 3,pp.3-19.

Dale, P. (1984) 'The danger within ourselves', *Community Care*, 501,pp.20-2.

Dale, P., Morrison, T., Davies, M., Noyes, P. and Roberts, W. (1983) 'A family therapy approach to child abuse: countering resistance', *Journal of Family Therapy*, 5,pp.117-44.

Davies, M. (1977) *Support Systems in Social Work*, London, Routledge & Kegan Paul.

Davies, M. (1981) *The Essential Social Worker (A guide to Positive Practice)*, London, Heinemann.

DHSS (1974) *Report of Committee of Enquiry into the Care and Supervision Provided by Local Authorities and Other Agencies in Relation to Maria Colwell and the Co-ordination Between Them*, London, HMSO.

DHSS (1982) *Child Abuse: A study of Enquiry Reports 1973-1981*.

Douglas, J. (1979) 'Behavioural work with families', *Journal of Family Therapy*, 1,pp.371-382.

Eisler, R.M. and Hersen, N. (1973) 'Behavioural techniques in family oriented crisis intervention', *Archives of General Psychiatry*, 28,pp.111-16.

Etherington, S. and Parker, C. (1982) 'In the still of the night', *Social Work Today*, 14,(5),pp.6-9.

Everstine, D.S., Bodin, A.M. and Everstine, L. (1977) 'Emergency Psychology: a mobile service for police crisis calls', *Family process*, 16,pp.281-92.

Fisher, M., Newton, E. and Sainsbury, E. (1984) *Mental Health Social Work Observed*, London, Allen & Unwin.

Forder, A. (1976) 'Social work and systems theory', *British Journal of Social Work*, 6,(1),pp.23-43.

Goffman, E. (1961) *Asylums*, London, Penguin.

Golan, N. (1978) *Treatment in Crisis Situations*, London, Free Press.

Goldberg, E.M, Warburton, W.R., McGuiness, B. and Rowlands, J.H. (1977) 'Towards Accountability in Social Work', *British*

Journal of Social Work,7,(3),pp.257-83.

Goldstein, H. (1973) *Social Work Practice: A Unitary Approach*, University of South Carolina Press.

Gorrell Barnes, G. (1980) 'Family Therapy in Social Work Setting: a survey by questionnaire 1976-1978', *Journal of Family Theray*, 2,pp.357-8.

Gorrel Barnes, G. (1984) *Working with Families*, London, Macmillan.

Gostick, C. and Scott, T. (1982) 'Local authority intake teams', *British Journal of Social Work*, 12,pp.395-421.

Green, S. (1982) 'Now I'm inclined to play it safe', *Community Care*, 11 November 1932,pp.19-20.

Grundy, E. (1982) 'An "out of hours" social work service in Tower Hamlets', *Social Work Service*, London, DHSS.

Guerin, P.J. (ed.) (1975) *Family Therapy*, New York, Gardner Press.

Haley, J. and Hoffman, L. (eds) (1967) *Techniques of Family Therapy*, New York, Basic Books Inc.

Hall, A.D. and Fagen, R.E. (1956) 'Definition of system', in Bertalanffy, L. von and Rapoport, A. (eds) *General Systems Year Book 1*, Society of General Systems Research.

Hill, R. (1958) 'Generic features of families under stress,' *Social Casework*, XXXIX,2-3. Reprinted in H.J. Parad (ed.) (1965) *Crisis Intervention: Selected Readings*, New York, Family Service Association of America, pp.32-52.

Hoffman, L. (1971) 'Deviation Amplifying Processes in Natural Groups', in Haley, J. (ed.) *Changing Families: A Family Therapy Reader*, New York, Grune & Stratton.

Janchill, St Mary P. (1969) 'Systems in Casework theory and practice', *Social Casework*, 50,(2), republished in Klenk, W. and Ryan, R.M. (eds) (1970) *The Practice of Social Work*, USA, Wadworth Publishing Co.

Jackson, D.D. (1957) 'The Question of Family Homeostasis', *Psychiatric Quarterly Supplement*, 31,pp.79 90.

Jenkins, J., Hilderbrand, J. and Lask, B. (1982) 'Failure: an exploration and survival kit', *Journal of Family Therapy*, 4,pp.307-20.

Jordan, W. (1972) *The Social Worker in Family Situations*, London, Routledge & Kegan Paul.

Jordan, W. (1974) *Poor Parents: Social Policy and the 'Cycle of Deprivation'*, London, Routledge & Kegan Paul.

Jordan, W. (1977) 'Against the unitary approach to social work', *New Society*, 2.6.77, pp.448-50.

Jordan, W. and Packman, J. (1978) 'Training for social work with violent families', in Martin, J.P. (ed.) *Violence in the Family*, Chichester, Wiley.

Jordan, W. (1981) 'Family therapy: an outsider's view', *Journal of Family Therapy*, 3,pp.269-80.

Jordan, W. (1984) 'Interview with Bill Jordan', *Social Work Today*, 16(1),10-14.

Kahn, J. and Earle, E. (1982) *The Cry for Help and the Professional Response*, Oxford, Pergamon.

Kew, S. (1975) *Handicap and Family Crisis*, London, Pitman.

Klein, D. and Ross, A. (1958) 'Kindergarten entry: A study of role transition', in Krugman, N. (ed.) *Orthopsychiatry and the School*, New York, American Orthopsychiatric Association. Reprinted in Parad, H.J. (ed.) *Crisis Intervention*, pp.140-8.

Knott, B.H. (1972) 'Social Conflict: Implications for Casework Practice', *British Journal of Social Work*, 2(4),pp.435-43.

Langsley, D.G., Pittman, F.S., Machotka, P. and Flomenhaft,K. (1968a) 'Family crisis therapy - results and implications, *Family Process*, 7,pp.753-9.

Langsley, D.G., Kaplan, D., Pittman, F.S., Machotka, P., Flomenhaft, K. and Deyoung, C. (1968b) *The Treatment of Families in Crisis*. New York, Grune & Stratton.

Langsley, D.G., Fairburn, R.H. and Deyoung, C. (1968c) 'Adolescence and family crisis', *Canadian Psychiatric Association Journal*, 13,pp.125-33.

Langsley, D.G., Machotka, P. and Flomenhaft, K. (1971) 'Avoiding mental hospital admission: a follow up study', *American Journal of Psychiatry*, 127 (10),pp.1391-4.

Le Masters, E.E. (1957) 'Parenthood as crisis' Reprinted from *Marriage and Family Living*, XIX(4), in Parad, H.J. (ed.) *Crisis Intervention*, pp.111-18.

Lindermann, E. (1944) 'Symptomatology and management of acute grief', *American Journal of Psychiatry*, 101. Reprinted in Parad, H.J. (ed.) *Crisis Intervention*, pp.7-21.

Loewenstein, C.L. (1974) 'An intake team in action in the social services department', *British Journal of Social Work*, 4(2),pp.115-41.

McGee, R.K. (1974) *Crisis Intervention in the Community*, Baltimore, University Park Press.

Maldanes, C. (1981) *Strategic Family Therapy*, San Francisco, Jossey-Bass.

Manor, O. (ed.) (1984) *Family Work in Action*, London, Tavistock.

Minuchin, S. (1974) *Families and Family Therapy*, London, Tavistock.

Minuchin, S. and Fishman, H.C. (1981) *Family Therapy Techniques*, Cambridge, USA, Harvard University Press.

Minuchin, S. and Montalvo, B. (1971) 'Techniques for working with disorganised low socioeconomic families', *American Journal of Orthopsychiatry*, 37,pp.880-7.

Moore, J. (1982) 'Like a rabbit caught in headlights', *Community Care*, 436,pp.18-20.

Morrice, J.K.W. (1976) *Crisis Intervention: Studies in Community Care*, Oxford, Pergamon.

O'Hagan, K.P. (1980a) 'Is social work necessary?' *Community Care*, 297,pp.24-6.

O'Hagan, K.P. (1980b) 'What if something terrible happened?' *Community Care*, 338,pp.16-18.

O'Hagan, K.P. (1983a) 'The story of Kerry', *Social Work Today*, 14(31),pp.10-15.

O'Hagan, K.P. (1983b) 'Not truth but persuasion', *Community Care*, 28.7.83,pp.14-17.

O'Hagan, K.P. (1984) 'Family crisis intervention in social services', *Journal of Family Therapy*, 6,pp.149-81.

Palazzoli, M.S., Cecchin, G., Prate, G. and Boscolo, L. (1978) *Paradox and Counterparadox*, New York, Jason Aronson.

Parad, H.J. (ed.) (1965) *Crisis Intervention: Selected Readings*, New York, Family Service Association of America.

Perlman, H.H. (1957) *Social Casework: A Problem Solving Process*, Chicago, University of Chicago Press.

Pinker, R.A. (1982) 'An Alternative view', in Barclay, P.M.*Social Workers*, pp.236-62.

Pittman, F.S. (1966) 'Techniques of family crisis therapy',in Masserman, J. (ed.) *Current psychiatric therapies*, New York, Grune & Stratton.

Pittman, F.S., Langsley, D.G., Flomenhaft, K., Deyoung, C.D., Machotka, P. and Kaplan, D.M. (1971) 'Therapy techniques of the family treatment unit, in J. Haley, (ed.) *Changing families: a family therapy Readex*, New York, Grune & Stratton, pp.259-70.

Pittman, F.S. (1973) 'Managing acute psychiatric emergencies. Defining the family crisis', in Bloch, D.A. (ed.) *Techniques of family psychotherapy*, New York, Grune & Stratton.

Plant, R. (1970) *Social and Moral Theory in Casework*, London, Routledge & Kegan Paul.

Puryear, D. (1979) *Helping People in Crisis*, California, Jossey Bass.

Rapoport, L. (1962) 'The state of crisis: some theoretical consideration', *Social Services Review*, XXXVI,2. Reprinted in H.J. Parad (ed.), *Crisis Intervention: Selected Readings*, New York, Family Service Association of America, pp.22-31.

Rapoport, L. (1971) 'Crisis intervention as a mode of brief treatment', in R.W. Roberts and R.H. Nee (eds), *Comparative Theories in Social Casework*, Chigago, University of Chigago Press, pp.267-311. Reprinted with minor changes in S.N. Katz (ed.) *Creativity in Social Work: Selected Writings of Lydia Rapoport*, Philadelphia, Temple University Press, pp.83-124.

Reading, P. (1983) 'An ever present nightmare', *Community Care*, 25.8.83,pp.19-21.

Schulberg, H.C. and Sheldon, A. (1968) 'Probabilities of crises and strategies for preventative intervention', *Archives of General Psychiatry*, vol. 18,pp.553-8.

Scott, D. (1974) 'Cultural frontiers in the Mental Health Service', *Schizophenia Bulletin*, pp.10.

Scott, D. and Starr, I. (1981) 'A 24 hour family oriented psychiatric and crisis service', *Journal of Family Therapy 3,pp.177-86.*

Skelt, A. (1983) 'Emergency duty', *Community Care*, 1,462,pp.19-22.

Skynner, A.C.R. (1979) 'Family therapist as family scapegoat', *Journal of Family Therapy*, 1,pp.7-22.

Speed, B., Seligman, P., Kingston, P. and Cade, B. (1982) 'A team approach to therapy', *Journal of Family Therapy*, 4,pp.271-84.

Speer, D.C. (1970) 'Family Systems: Morphostasis and Morphogenesis', *Family Process*, 9(3)pp.260-75.

Stratham, D. (1978) *Radicals in Social Work*, London, Routledge & Kegan Paul.

Stratford, J., Burck, C. and Kingston, W. (1982) 'The influence of context on the assessment of family interaction: a clinical study', *Journal of Family Therapy*, 4,pp.359-71.

Szasz, T.S. (1972) *The Myth of Mental Illness*, Paladin, Herts, England.

Timms, N. (1964) *Social Casework: Principles and Practice*, London, Routledge & Keegan Paul.

Timms, N. (1983) *Social Work Values: an enquiry*, London, Routledge & Kegan Paul.

Titmuss, R.M. (1965) 'Goals of Today's Welfare State', in P. Anderson and R. Blackburn (eds) *Towards Socialism*, London, Fontana.

Tower Hamlets (1982) *Children who Come into Care in Tower Hamlets*, London, Borough of Tower Hamlets.

Umana, M.S. Gross, S.J., and McConville, M.T. (1980) *Crisis in the Family: Three Approaches*, New York, Gardner.

Vickery, A. (1974) 'A systems approach to social work intervention: its uses for work with individuals and families', *British Journal of Social Work*, 4(4),pp. 389-404.

Walrond-Skinner, S. (1976) *Family Therapy: The Treatment of Natural Systems*, London, Routledge & Kegan Paul.

Walrond-Skinner, S. (1984) 'Whither family therapy? Twenty years on', *Journal of Family Therapy*, 6,pp.1-16.

Wadzlawick, P., Beavin, J. and Jackson, D. (1967) *Pragmatics of Human Communication*, New York, Norton.

Whan, M. (1983) 'Tricks of the trade: questionable theory and practice in family therapy', *British Journal of Social Work*, 13(1),pp.321-37.

Whitaker, C. (1973) 'My philosophy of psychotherapy', *Journal of Contempoary Psychotherapy*, 6,pp.49-52.

Witt, K.N. De (1978) The effectiveness of family therapy, *Archives of General Psychiatry*, 35,pp.549-61.

Wilding, P. (1982) *Professional Power and Social Welfare*, London, Routledge & Kegan Paul.

Wright, C. (1981) 'The quickness of the hand deceives the eye', *Community Care*, 377,pp.20-1.

Younghusband, E. (1967) *Social Work and Social Values*, London, Allen & Unwin.

Index

Ackerman, N. 58, 113
Aguilera, D.C. 16, 143
American psychiatry 15-21, 39
  perceptions of social
  workers 16, 39
'armchair casework
  morality' 106, 110, 112, 115
authority 111, 118

Barclay, P.M. 49
Barnet 21
Beirut 29
Bertalanffy, L. von 66
Biestek, F. 106, 112
Bleasdale, A. 44
Boszormenji-Nagy, I. 58
Bott, E. 21, 48, 49
'Boys from the Blackstuff' 44
British Association of Social
  Workers 10
Brixton, 15
Buckle, J. 9
Butler, A. 19

Cade, B. 58
Caplan, G. 15, 17 – 19, 29, 57
casework relationship 106
child abuse 1 – 6, 22, 25 – 6, 28
Clark, J. 7
classical crisis literature 14, 15,
  39, 57, 114
client perceptions 24, 41, 42, 43
community workers 140
control 111 – 14, 117
Cooklin, A. 58

crisis
  as system 61 – 6, 89
  attraction of 8, 19
  conceptual framework 35 – 8
  conflictual nature of 29 – 30,
    86, 107 – 8, 117
  definition 13, 14, 15, 141
  in community 45, 82, 107
  invoking statutory powers 29,
    113
  participants 29
  perceptions of 8, 14
  referrals 30 – 3, 83, 122
  rescuing clients from 27 – 9
  research of 19, 122 – 3,
  resolution of 101
  theory of 17, 19
  therapeutic potential of 19,
    56, 101
  violence in 109
crisis intervention
  definition 140
  emergence of 15
  goals of 142
  pioneers in 15 – 21, 39, 114,
    139
  principles of 28, 129 – 32,
    134 – 5

Davies, M. 49, 59, 119
DHSS 10
double bind, 100
Douglas, J. 58

Earle, E. 118

Eisler, R.M. 58
emergency duty teams 10, 11
emergency psychiatric
    admissions 15

Fagen, R.E. 62
family crisis intervention 13,
    20, 56
family therapy 21, 55
    criticism of
        techniques 116 – 17
    literature 57
    principles 56
    techniques 56, 88
    theories 58 – 60
    use of space 89 – 93
Fishman, H.C. 57
Forder, A. 59, 61
Framo, J. 58

Goffman, E. 48
Goldstein, H. 59
Gorrell Barnes, G. 109

Hall, A.D. 62
Hersen, N. 58
Hill, R. 59
Hoffman, L. 57, 59

inalienable rights 107
intake teams 9, 10
IT 8

Jackson, D.D. 57
Janchill, M. 59
Jordan, W. 7, 60, 106, 108,
    115, 116

Kahn, J. 118
Klein, D. 15

Langsley, D.G. 14, 17, 20, 21,
    56
Le Masters, E.E. 16
Lindermann, E. 16
Loewenstein, C.L. 9

Maldanes, C. 58
manipulation 112 – 14
manipulative techniques 107

'Maria Colwell' 10, 134
media 43
Messick, J.N. 16
Mental Health Act 8
Minuchin, S. 57, 58, 59
Moore, J. 119, 126

Napsbury hospital. 46
NHS 51

O'Hagan, K.P. 50, 57, 95,
    103, 128

Packman, J. 7, 108, 109,
    115, 116
Palazzoli, M.S. 58
perceptual intervention 69, 70
Perlman, H.H. 118, 119
Pinker, R.A 119
Pittman, F.S. 62, 114
Pizzey, E. 29
Plant, R. 106
plea-for-removal crises 41
    characteristics of 41
    clamour for removal 44 – 7
    definition 40
    description 22, 40, 41
    increase in 51, 129
power, 110 – 14
preventative community
    psychiatry 15, 16
Pritchard, C. 19

Rapaport, L. 17, 20, 57, 119
recording 127
role play 8
Ross, A. 15

Seebohm 9, 10, 16
Schulberg, H.C. 14
Scott, D. 21
Sheldon, A. 14
Skynner, R. 128
social services 9, 12, 13, 16,
    32, 34, 39, 40, 43, 45, 47,
    51, 55, 58, 59, 69, 80, 119,
    122
    crisis service 21 – 3, 33

open door policy   30 – 1
perceptions of   46, 52, 53
senior management   44,
    128 – 33
social work teams   123
team leaders   121, 123, 126
    127
social workers
  crisis tasks   21 – 3, 33
  limitations of   124
  middle class   29, 115, 119
      142
  moral vulnerability of   73 – 80
      88 – 9, 94 – 7
  perceptions of   16, 24, 35 – 8
      42, 71
  potential of   12
  relation to clients   106
  supervision of   125 – 6, 129
  self-knowledge   53, 58, 71,
      74 – 9, 89, 94 – 7, 138 – 9
  untrained for crisis   11, 52
Speed, B.   109
Starr, I.   21
system theory   58, 59 – 66,
    86 – 8, 93 – 4

closed system   62
'equilibrium'   65
homeostasis   64 – 6
morphogenesis and
    morphostasis   63 – 6, 67 – 8
    70
negative feedback   64, 87
open system   62, 86
positive feedback   64
steady state   64 – 5

Timms, N.   016, 119
Titmuss, R.M.   106

Umana, M.S.   14, 56

Vickery, A.   59

Walrond-Skinner, S.   58, 63,
    111
Watzlawick, P.   58
welfare rights   8
Whan, M.   106, 107, 116 – 17
Wilding, P.   116
Wright, C.   107

Younghusband, E.   106, 119